Blood
Moon

SAT Vocabulary Prep Novel

K. J. Gillenwater

Cover art design by K. J. Gillenwater
Photograph by andreiuc88
Wolf silhouette by Earthen-wolf-spirit from DeviantArt

First print publication: September 2015

ABOUT THIS BOOK

This book contains 1000 SAT words to build your vocabulary as you read. These words are underlined and numbered throughout the text to identify them. A definition for each word appears in the footnotes.

PROLOGUE

"Come on, Jenna." Jake Tanner tugged the hand of the petite blonde standing beside him.

"I don't know, Jake." Jenna Tinsley hesitated. "Are you sure there's a party way out here?"

The two teenagers stood at the edge of a thick forest. In the dark, the tangle of tree limbs and underbrush made an impregnable[1] wall.

His grip tightened. "Don't you trust me?"

Jenna's date for the evening was agile[2], broad-shouldered, and captain of the football team at Northeast High. For weeks she'd hoped he would ask her out. Now, here they were, in the middle of nowhere on their way to some bonfire party. She quickly dispelled[3] any fears she had. "Of course I trust you." She squeezed his hand.

He smiled widely.

Jenna started. In the moonlight, his teeth were resplendent[4], glittering bright white, and unusually pointed. She'd never noticed that before. Her imagination and the darkness must be playing tricks on her. Honestly. Pointy teeth? She smiled as they entered the forest. Jake Tanner had asked her out. She should be over the moon and not questioning the sharpness of his teeth.

---

[1] Impregnable – impossible to enter by force

[2] Agile – quick in movement; nimble

[3] Dispelled – to drive away or cause to disappear

[4] Resplendent – very bright

Jake led her into the heart of the woods. They wound through the trees and bushes, taking a circuitous[5] route.

Branches pulled at her hair, and raspberry canes pricked through her jeans. "How much farther is it?" She had dressed carefully for her date. Now she probably looked as if she'd been through a hurricane or something.

What kind of idiots had a party way out here?

Jake didn't answer her. Instead, he pulled her along faster, over rocks and through shallow streams. They moved at a frenetic[6] pace.

"Jake, I said I'm getting tired." She attempted to yank free of his grasp, but his grip was solid. "Let's go back to the car."

"We're almost there."

She trembled at the raspy, low timbre[7] of his voice. Trepidation[8] squeezed her heart. Her earlier joy from being asked out by such a popular guy dissipated. She was in the middle of nowhere with a football player who outweighed her by at least a hundred pounds. What if there *was* no party? What if Jake had something else in mind?

Through the veil of branches, Jenna caught sight of the orange glow of a fire. Relief poured in. A fire meant a party. A party meant people. They weren't alone after all.

They broke through the trees into a clearing. Her relief vanished when around the fire she noticed a dearth[9] of people. Something definitely did not seem right. "I don't know. I think I want to go back."

"It's too late to go back," someone said behind her.

Jenna screamed and clung tremulously[10] to her date.

Who was that?

Jake laughed without even a modicum[11] of sympathy. "Geez, Jenna, it's just Carter."

---

[5] Circuitous - roundabout

[6] Frenetic – frenzied, hectic, frantic

[7] Timbre – the distinctive property of a complex sound

[8] Trepidation – a state of alarm or dread, apprehension

[9] Dearth – a scarce supply, a lack

[10] Tremulously – timid or fearful

[11] Modicum – a small, moderate, or token amount

Carter Rittenhouse, Jake's best friend, stepped out from behind a copse[12] of trees. "Come on." He amicably[13] beckoned them toward the fire. "We've been waiting for you guys."

The beat of Jenna's heart abated[14], slowing to a dull thud. There really *was* a party after all. Jake had told the truth. After smoothing back her hair Jenna walked into the clearing where the fire blazed. Being here with Jake meant she'd joined the popular crowd. When she went back to school on Monday, everything would be different. No more lunches at the geek table. Now she was one of them.

Her date pushed her closer to the fire.

A weird, scratched out circle surrounded her, as if someone had taken a stick and carefully drawn the figure there in the dirt. "What's this?" She looked over her shoulder, and Jake had disappeared. "Jake?" The night grew colder, and she stuck her hands into the pockets of her coat.

From this desolate[15] spot in the woods, she heard only the wind rattling through the trees. She shivered. The quiet unnerved her. "Jake!" She spun around in the circle. He wouldn't leave her here all alone, would he? She had no idea how to get back to his car. He would have to come back for her.

The wind blew stronger, but this time it carried a dissonant[16] mix of mumbling voices and high-pitched whines. She covered her ears at the unearthly blend of sounds. The noises crept nearer. Panic set in. She had to get out of here.

"Jake!" She hoped her voice could be heard over the cacophony[17]--howling, grunting, even screeching. Fraught[18] with terror, she didn't want to leave the fire. Its orange and yellow flames were comforting in the darkness.

The noise closed in from all around her, incessant[19],

---

[12] Copse – thicket of small trees or shrubs

[13] Amicably – friendly

[14] Abated – reduced, lessened

[15] Desolate - deserted

[16] Dissonant – harsh and inharmonious in sound

[17] Cacophony – tremendous noise

[18] Fraught – filled or accompanied

[19] Incessant - unending

3

growing ever louder. Who made those noises? She would go mad if they didn't shut up. Tears welled up in her eyes.

Abruptly, the racket ended and an absolute quiet surrounded her. No wind, no animal sounds. Nothing. A faint rustling noise in the trees caught her attention. "Jake, is that you?" She wiped her tears with the sleeve of her coat.

"We're all here, Jenna." A figure came forward out of the gloom. "We've been waiting for you." Green eyes glowed malevolently[20] in the dark.

Jenna took a step back toward the fire.

Black shapes with faces obscured[21] emerged from the woods. She searched for her date among them. Jake had to be there somewhere. As the black figures came closer a noisome[22] odor, like rotted meat, emanated[23] from them. Jenna gasped at the foul smell.

The figure who had spoken came closer, and Jenna noticed flames reflected in dark-rimmed glasses. She knew those glasses.

"You." She pointed an accusatory[24] and trembling finger. "What are you doing here?"

"Come now, Jenna." The figure crept closer to her. "Why don't you get back in the circle? We've got a long night ahead of us."

Jenna stumbled backward. The dark shapes eased out of the shadows of the forest, closing in on her.

"Jake!" This wasn't a party. Why didn't he help her? She tripped over a stone and fell into the dirt. Claws reached forward and grabbed her by the arms.

Claws?

Fright enervated[25] her—her arms were flaccid[26] and her legs were immobile. Before she could process anything more, razor teeth sank into her shoulder with a sharp stab of pain and everything went dark.

---

[20] Malevolently – maliciously, evilly
[21] Obscured – to conceal in obscurity, hide
[22] Noisome – offensive, foul
[23] Emanate – to come forth, as from a source
[24] Accusatory – containing or implying accusation
[25] Enervated – to weaken or destroy the vitality of
[26] Flaccid – lacking firmness, resilience, or muscle tone

CHAPTER ONE

Ms. Woodlawn didn't allow any talking in her immaculate[27] and well-organized library at Northeast High School. But Dina Moore couldn't help herself, the gossip was just too good. "Did you hear what happened to Jenna Tinsley?" She eagerly leaned forward. Her trademark dangly earrings jingled with every excited bob of her brunette head.

"Oh, Dina, can't you keep your mind on our physics homework?" Dina's best friend, Savannah Black, tapped her pencil on the copious[28] piles of books and papers in front of them.

"Just because you're gunning for valedictorian is no reason for me to work like a dog my senior year," Dina huffed. "Come on, back me up on this, Nick."

Nick Bishop eyed both girls. In a conundrum[29], he appeared troubled about which side to take. He always ended up in the middle when dissent[30] came between the girls, but he must've been curious about Jenna Tinsley. The look on his face convinced Dina his curiosity needed to be satiated[31].

"I overheard in Mr. Dickerson's class first period that Jenna's been missing since last Friday!" Dina couldn't suppress[32]

---

[27] Immaculate – impeccably clean, spotless
[28] Copious – large in quantity, abundant
[29] Conundrum – a dilemma
[30] Dissent – disagreement, difference of opinion or feeling
[31] Satiated – to satisfy fully
[32] Suppress – to inhibit the expression of

her excitement at the enigmatic[33] disappearance of her classmate.

Savannah, her russet curls partially concealing her face, leaned over her physics textbook. Her mouth formed a line, revealing disapproval of the idle gossip that ruled Dina's life most of the time. Although the girls were best friends, they didn't see eye to eye on every topic.

Nick chimed in. "That makes three kids missing since school started, and it's only the end of September."

Dina's heart skipped a happy beat when Nick took the bait. "I know, and Principal Morgan hasn't said a word to the PTA about it."

"How do you know that?" Savannah was clearly aggravated[34] by how easily Dina pulled their focus away from school work and, instead, propagated[35] some item from the Northeast rumor mill.

"My mother went to the first meeting of the year, after Carter Rittenhouse and Jake Tanner disappeared. When one of the parents brought it up, Principal Morgan dismissed it as nothing more than a senior prank."

"But Carter's a junior." Nick closed his English textbook and set it to the side.

"I know. You would think someone would have called him on that." Dina doodled idly on her notebook cover. Her sketch of Principal Morgan took shape as she talked. He had a round potato face and wore silly aviator frame glasses. She knew Savannah found it nauseating[36] how easily drawing came to her.

"Ahem."

All three jumped at the noise. Ms. Woodlawn hovered right over their work table. Dina tucked her notebook into her backpack so that Ms. Woodlawn wouldn't see her work.

"Sorry, Ms. Woodlawn," whispered Savannah.

Dina knew this was Savannah's favorite study spot after school. Ticking off the librarian the year they all graduated would not be a good idea. Dina folded her hands and bit her lip doing her

---

[33] Enigmatic - puzzling

[34] Aggravated – to arouse to exasperation or anger

[35] Propagate – to make widely known, publicize

[36] Nauseating – causing disgust, loathing, or revulsion

best to look contrite[37].

Nick followed Savannah's lead, "Yeah, we're sorry."

Ms. Woodlawn sniffed at the aberration[38] of three loud students in her quiet library, tucked a piece of loose hair into her tight chignon, and strode back to her stool behind the check-out counter. Ms. Woodlawn had only begun working at the library a few years ago, but since her arrival she'd removed clutter, organized the stacks, and made it known she had no tolerance for talkers. As Savannah had noted during their first study session in the library as freshmen, silence and structure in a place of learning was sacrosanct[39] to the librarian.

Dina rolled her eyes in vexation[40] and sketched a picture of a dragon that looked decidedly like the recently departed librarian.

Nick rolled a pencil back and forth across the spiky blonde hair on top of his head—one of his dilatory[41] habits when attempting to study. With a dour[42] expression, he scanned his pile of notes and returned to his homework.

Savannah scribbled furiously on a piece of loose leaf paper and slid it to the middle of the table for both of her friends to see:

LET'S TALK LATER

Savannah viewed most school gossip as fatuous[43] amusement that detracted[44] from her studies. Dina knew, however, the minute she divulged[45] Jenna as one of the missing students that Savannah would want to know more.

Jenna Tinsley and Savannah had both been actively pursuing the goal of valedictorian since freshman year. They had a genial[46] rivalry Dina could trace back to junior high. One week Jenna would score an A+ on her math quiz. Next week Savannah

---

[37] Contrite – feeling regret or sorrow for one's sins or offenses

[38] Aberration – a departure from the normal or typical

[39] Sacrosanct – regarded as sacred or inviolable

[40] Vexation – irritation or annoyance

[41] Dilatory – tending to postpone or delay

[42] Dour – silently ill-humored, gloomy

[43] Fatuous – vacuous, mindless

[44] Detracted – Drew or took away from, diverted

[45] Divulged – Made known

[46] Genial – having a pleasant or friendly disposition or manner

would receive a perfect score on her English exam. Over the weekend, Jenna should've been studying for the big American History test they took this morning.

Interesting that Savannah hadn't noticed Jenna's absence in class. Did Mr. Slatterly even take attendance today? Dina couldn't remember. But Jenna had never taken a hiatus[47] on the day of a test. Not since Dina had known her.   Savannah's brows knit together as they returned to their studying. Perhaps, at first, Savannah viewed Jenna's disappearance as a piece of innocuous gossip. Now Dina could see determination and curiosity had set in and knew her best friend wouldn't let go of this bit of news so easily.

*

"How are you feeling, Jenna?"

The unfamiliar voice rasped in the darkness and jolted Jenna awake.

When had she fallen asleep? Why wasn't she home in bed?

As her mind cleared, memories inundated[48] her: Jake taking her deep into the woods, the bonfire, and then…

Her skin crawled at the lurid[49] memory of the shadowy figures lurching out of the woods toward her, and then the pain.

Her shoulder and neck ached horribly, and she reached up to feel the spot. She was repulsed[50] when she touched a warm stickiness. She jerked her hand away. The stickiness felt like blood, but the dim lighting made it impossible to see anything more than the silhouetted outline of her fingers.

What had happened out in the woods? Was she bleeding from some kind of laceration[51]? She couldn't remember. Her mind had grown fuzzy. As she attempted to sit up, she sensed something ponderous[52] attached to her ankle. She pulled and felt resistance. A chain had been clamped around her lower leg. A scream built in her throat.

---

[47] Hiatus – a break

[48] Inundated - overwhelmed

[49] Lurid – causing shock and horror, gruesome

[50] Repulsed – driven back, repelled

[51] Laceration – a jagged wound or cut

[52] Ponderous – unwieldy from weight or bulk

"You're safe. You're okay. I'm here to take care of you," her interlocutor[53] in the dark soothed.

Jenna couldn't tell if the growly, low voice was male or female. She wanted to know why she was fettered[54], but her mouth had grown parched. Perplexed[55] and scared, she attempted to call out for Jake, but she could only manage a groan.

"The first few days are the hardest, but then it becomes much easier." The voice moved closer to her.

First few days of what?

Jenna wanted to go home. She wanted Jake to come get her and take her back home to the bed waiting in her bedroom. Something lightly touched her on the knee. She jerked away. The pain in her shoulder was acute[56] and she cowered in defeat.

"Relax." The touch returned. "I know it hurts, but I can't dress the wound. It needs to heal on its own."

This time Jenna relaxed. She pretended not to be scared out of her wits. Until she could figure out more about where she was and who held her, keeping her sanity might be the only thing to save her. First, she needed to come to terms with the idea of being shackled in a strange, dark place. Then, she could work on an escape plan.

"I'm sorry we have to chain you, but it's necessary. You'll see." The voice had noticeable empathy[57]. "Are you thirsty? I can give you water. The Master allows water and nothing more."

The Master?

She was very thirsty, and the thought of water pushed all worries and fears out of her mind. She groaned, hoping that would be enough to let the voice know she desperately needed a drink.

"I'll be right back."

A strange shuffling sound came out of the inky blackness. She tried to discern[58] who moved across the room. Jenna shivered at the sound.

---

[53] Interlocutor – someone who takes part in a conversation

[54] Fettered – a chain or shackle for the ankles or feet

[55] Perplexed – filled with confusion or bewilderment

[56] Acute – extremely sharp or severe, intense

[57] Empathy –understanding of another's situation or feelings

[58] Discern – to perceive with the eyes or intellect, detect

A sliver of yellow light appeared. A door stood not twenty feet from where she lay. An accessible[59] escape! Jenna's heart skipped a beat at that new bit of knowledge.

Her heart almost stopped, however, when she caught a glimpse of something terrifying. Something heinous[60] made her blood run cold. A hand gripped the doorknob, but not a human hand. The soothing voice had not been human at all. The hand was hirsute[61], covered in long brown hair, its nails yellow and curving like tiny scimitars.

Jenna recoiled[62] against the wall and screamed. She found her voice and used it as best she could.

The animal-like hand gripped the doorknob. "Turn off the light, idiot!" the voice snarled.

The yellow light that had given Jenna hope snapped off in an instant. The memory of that hairy, clawed hand burned in her brain. Who or what kept her captive in this dark, frigid[63] room?

A paroxysm[64] of anger bloomed inside her—virulent[65], animalistic, uncontrollable. It felt good to be angry. The anger gave her weak body strength. This time she screamed not in fear, but in rage. Whoever did this to her would pay. She screamed once more, and it came out like a growl this time—feral[66] and raw. Power surged through her limbs, and she strained against the chain holding her ankle captive.

She would show her captors she was someone to be feared. Give her the opportunity to show them, and she would. Just wait.

*

Savannah knocked on the Tinsley's' front door waiting for someone to answer.

She'd stayed at the school library until it closed at six

[59] Accessible – easily approached or entered
[60] Heinous – grossly wicked or reprehensible
[61] Hirsute – covered with hair
[62] Recoiled – shrank back in fear or repugnance
[63] Frigid – extremely cold
[64] Paroxysm – a sudden outburst of emotion or action
[65] Virulent – bitterly hostile or antagonistic
[66] Feral – existing in a wild or untamed state

o'clock. Nick and Dina were long gone, as usual. Savannah always studied harder and longer than her two friends. Tonight, however, her concentration had been shaken by the story of her missing rival. At first, she'd thought Dina's gossip about Jenna and the other missing students was inane[67]. But as she drove her Corolla home from school, she found herself pulling up in front of Jenna's house. Jenna's parents would certainly have more information than a couple of high school kids relying on rumors.

She'd been waiting on the front porch for five minutes, and still no one had answered the door. She knocked again, harder this time. The Tinsleys lived in a massive[68] house in the ritzier section of Centerville. Maybe they were upstairs and couldn't hear her pounding on the heavy oak double doors.

The door opened.

A prim-looking woman appeared in the doorway. Mrs. Tinsley was impeccable[69] in a dark pantsuit, wedge heels, and a long strand of what could only be real pearls. She'd carefully curled and styled her hair. This didn't appear to be a distraught[70] parent of a missing teenage girl.

Relief flooded her. Dina's story had only been a rumor. Jenna was fine. Savannah surmised[71] she must be safe at home recuperating[72] from a flu bug or something. She smiled.

"Yes? May I help you?" Mrs. Tinsley didn't recognize her.

It had been a few years since Savannah's last after school visit. In junior high she and Jenna had been much closer. Not best friends close, but they would do marathon study sessions at each other's homes. Savannah believed in the old adage of keeping friends close, but your enemies closer.

"Uh, hi, I'm Savannah. Savannah Black?" Her mind flipped through plausible reasons for stopping by. "I'm, uh, here to drop off Jenna's homework assignments from school today." She gestured at her heavy backpack slung over her shoulder.

---

[67] Inane – lacks sense or substance

[68] Massive – large or imposing

[69] Impeccable – having no flaws, perfect

[70] Distraught – deeply agitated, as from emotional conflict

[71] Surmised – made a guess or conjecture

[72] Recuperating – returning to health, recovering

"Homework?" Mrs. Tinsley seemed puzzled by Savannah's appearance on her porch.

"Yes, we share a couple of the same classes. I knew she wouldn't want to get behind, especially not so early in the year, so I took it upon myself to get extra copies of the assignments." It wasn't true, but she could certainly whip something up once she got up to Jenna's bedroom. Then, she could see Jenna for herself, get the details, and report back to Dina. She wanted to quell[73] the rumor about Jenna's disappearance as quickly as possible.

"Well, I don't know why she would need any assignments. She's on the senior class trip to Washington D.C." Mrs. Tinsley looked pointedly at Savannah, most likely wondering why she wasn't on the class trip, too. "She left last Friday afternoon. She should be back late tonight. I think one of her classmates is dropping her off around ten o'clock."

"Senior class trip?" Savannah echoed, disheartened[74] and confused. What trip? Something was going on, but until she could ascertain[75] the truth, it didn't make any sense to worry Jenna's mother. "Oh, yeah. Right. I forgot. My mom wouldn't sign the permission form." She hoped her excuse sounded plausible[76].

Mrs. Tinsley gave her a pitying look.

"You say she'll be back tonight?"

"Yes, that's what the form said. That boy had been kind enough to offer to give Jenna a ride home. Saves us the trouble."

"Oh." Savannah didn't know what to think. Who was 'that boy' who would be dropping Jenna off at home? She needed to elicit[77] the answer to that question. "Who was going to give her a ride?"

Mrs. Tinsley looked at her oddly, and Savannah didn't blame her. Kind of a strange question to ask. What did it really matter who dropped her off? But Savannah felt in her bones this was an important piece of information to find out.

"Hmm. I think his name was Jack or Jake, or something

---

[73] Quell – to suppress

[74] Disheartened – made less hopeful or enthusiastic

[75] Ascertain – to discover with certainty

[76] Plausible – seemingly acceptable or credible

[77] Elicit – to bring or draw out

like that. He was really quite gentlemanly. He picked up Jenna after school last Friday, too, so they could get on the bus together for the trip." Mrs. Tinsley displayed an ephemeral[78] smile at that recollection. "I think he may have a bit of a crush on our Jenna." She played with the pearls around her throat.

Could she mean Jake Tanner? Could the other missing student be the linchpin[79] to this mystery? Something weird definitely was going on at Northeast High, but what exactly? To Savannah, Jenna skipping school had been an anomaly[80]. Jenna definitely wasn't the kind to be clandestinely[81] dating a football player.

Mrs. Tinsley closed the door. Savannah wondered if any part of the rumor included a faked permission slip or Jake. Tomorrow she'd have to track Dina down at school and find out.

---

[78] Ephemeral – lasting for a markedly brief time
[79] Linchpin – a central, cohesive element
[80] Anomaly – deviation or departure from the normal
[81] Clandestinely – kept or done in secret

13

CHAPTER TWO

"She was with Jake Tanner?" Dina asked <u>skeptically</u>[82] while sitting in the cafeteria picking at her tray of gelatinous food.

"That's what she said." Savannah opened up the paper bag that held her lunch. "Supposedly he picked her up for a senior class field trip." The <u>meager</u>[83] <u>edible</u>[84] offerings at the school cafeteria made food from home seem like four-star cuisine. Her tuna sandwich and pretzels looked much more appetizing than the mystery meat <u>congealing</u>[85] on Dina's tray.

"But there's no field trip," Nick pointed out. He had loaded his tray with three rolls, several packets of peanut butter, and an apple.

"Nick, sometimes you can be so dense," Dina chided him, rolling her eyes.

Nick flamed red at making such an <u>inept</u>[86] statement. "What I meant to say was…"

"We know what you meant." Savannah shot Dina a look that said 'back off.' She really liked Nick a lot, and hated how Dina teased him so <u>mercilessly</u>[87] sometimes. He was a nice guy who

---

[82] Skeptically – in a manner that is marked by or given to doubt

[83] Meager – deficient in quantity, scanty

[84] Edible – fit to be eaten

[85] Congealing – coagulating or jelling

[86] Inept – not apt or fitting, inappropriate

[87] Mercilessly – having no mercy, cruel

could be inarticulate[88] from time to time. Nice guys were a rare commodity[89] in this school.

Savannah glanced over at the jock table. Take those guys, for instance, all muscles and over-moussed hair. Somehow the popular crowd encompassed[90] guys like them. Carter Rittenhouse caught her eye, his tall frame standing out in the crowd. Not only was he a star on the football team, but his height gave him an advantage in basketball, too. Savannah ruminated[91] while chewing her sandwich.

"Hey, Dina." Savannah nudged her friend in the side. Dina put down her fork mid-bite. "It's Carter!"

Carter was one of the missing kids Dina mentioned yesterday. Seemed he wasn't missing anymore.

"Where?" Dina made a cursory[92] glance around the cafeteria.

"Right there." Savannah pushed her friend's head gently in the right direction.

"Oh my God." Dina gaped. "It *is* him."

"Didn't he and Jake disappear about the same time?" Nick turned to get a look at Carter, too.

"Yeah. The Friday after school started—poof!" Dina flicked her fingers as if she'd completed a magic trick. "Gone. And no one said a word. Well, the principal didn't anyway. Where do you suppose he's been all this time?"

Savannah swallowed a bite of her sandwich. "I don't know, but he's back now. Could he have been sick or something?"

"I don't think so." Nick turned his attention back to his food. "My mom works at the hospital, remember? She would've said something to me if someone from school was *that* sick."

"Right." Dina, screwed her lips sideways, clearly thinking hard about the possibilities.

Carter acted like his normal arrogant[93] self, tripping the

---

[88] Inarticulate – unable to speak with clarity or eloquence

[89] Commodity – something that can be turned into an advantage

[90] Encompassed – constituted, included

[91] Ruminating – turning a matter over and over in the mind

[92] Cursory – performed with haste and scant attention to detail

[93] Arrogant – having a sense of overbearing self-importance

freshman as they walked by with full trays of food and sidling up to the popular girls at the table next to his to flirt. Carter Rittenhouse was the <u>antithesis</u>[94] of Nick. Even though he'd been missing for days, Carted acted as if he'd been here all along.

"It doesn't make any sense." Savannah took a swig of milk.

"Have any of you seen Jake or Jenna today?" Nick asked. "Maybe all three of them were together over the weekend."

It stood to reason that if Carter had returned, maybe Jake and Jenna had too.

"Not me." Dina <u>grimaced</u>[95] after tasting the mystery meat in front of her and pushed her tray away. All that remained was her carton of milk. She set it in front of her as if she were a <u>gourmand</u>[96] about to dine on a five-course meal.

"Me neither," said Savannah. "But I don't have any classes with Jake or Carter."

"Yeah, me neither, now that I think about it." Dina took small sips of milk as if she were trying to make it last as long as possible. "What about Jenna? Isn't she in Chess Club?" Chess Club held meetings every Monday during lunch.

"I think so." As a science <u>fanatic</u>[97], Nick usually participated in anything related to math or science. He didn't belong to the Chess Club, but he had a few friends that did.

"Jenna's in my sixth period class," Savannah said. "I'll let you know if I see her there."

"Seems kind of weird to put Jake and Jenna together, doesn't it?" Dina asked.

Dina was right. The few girls in the Chess Club weren't the type who would hang out with <u>puissant</u>[98] boys from the football team. Jenna wasn't unattractive, but she'd be an <u>atypical</u>[99] date for the high school football star. Those guys usually stuck with the cheerleaders.

---

[94] Antithesis – the direct or exact opposite

[95] Grimaced – sharp contorting of the face in pain or disgust

[96] Gourmand – a lover of good food

[97] Fanatic – a person marked by an extreme, unreasoning enthusiasm

[98] Puissant - powerful

[99] Atypical – unusual or irregular

"Maybe they weren't together," Savannah speculated[100]. "The fact that Carter and Jake disappeared on the same night might mean absolutely nothing." She grew tired of the conversation. Yes, it was strange Carter had returned, but he appeared to be fine. Just because a rumor was floating around didn't mean it was true.

Nick polished off his third and final roll slathered in peanut butter. He took a long drink of milk from the carton. "But Jenna's still missing."

Dina beset[101] upon that statement in an instant. "Yeah, she is. This weird 'senior trip' thing smells fishy to me. Something isn't right."

Savannah crumpled up her paper bag. "Well, something isn't right with the fact that I have a Spanish quiz next period, and I'm not studying." She got up and tossed her bag in the closest garbage can.

"Can't you think about anything besides class, Savannah?" Dina followed her out the door of the cafeteria into the hall. Nick was close behind them.

"Not when my grades will decide whether I get into Harvard or Centerville Community College." Savannah headed toward the library. Spanish started in ten minutes, which gave her enough time for a plenary[102] review of the vocab and grammar concepts.

Dina rolled her eyes and jangled her earrings. "Like you wouldn't get into Harvard."

Savannah challenged her spurious[103] claim, "Just because I have a 4.0, doesn't mean I'll get into Harvard." The Ivy League school was in her plan, but who knew if that plan would come to fruition[104]? There were too many unknown variables[105] this early in her senior year to guarantee her a spot at Harvard.

"Doesn't hurt, though," said Nick. They stopped at the door to the library. "I gotta go. See you guys later." Nick headed

---

[100] Speculated – meditated on a subject, thought

[101] Beset – attack on all sides

[102] Plenary – complete in all respects

[103] Spurious – not genuine, false

[104] Fruition – realization of something desired, accomplishment

[105] Variable – something that changes or is prone to changing

down the corridor that led to his locker.

Dina watched him walk down the hall.

"He's a cutie, isn't he?" Dina looked expectantly at Savannah to corroborate[106] her declaration.

Savannah felt the heat of a blush in her cheeks at the artless[107] comment. Nick was only fifteen feet away from them. She shushed her friend. "He's just a friend—a nice one. Let's keep that way, shall we?"

"Oh, come on." Dina nudged her in the side. "It's patently[108] obvious how much he changed since last year. He must've grown four or five inches since last June."

The horrible thing was, Savannah *had* noticed. Nick was a good friend, not to mention a great study partner. She didn't want to mess that up by mooning over him in class. She certainly didn't need a distraction like him her last year of high school.

Nick was sweet. Nick was nice. And, yes, Nick was cute. But Savannah couldn't think about that now. She wanted to eschew[109] the topic, frankly. Her focus returned to the Spanish quiz. "Look, I would love to stay and chat about all things Nick, but I really want to study, okay?"

Dina, exasperated[110], threw up her hands and headed back to the cafeteria to find other friends before the bell rang. As Dina walked away, Savannah couldn't help thinking about Jenna and Jake and why they would be together. Something didn't add up.

*

"Ms. Woodlawn, I hope you concur[111] with me on this."

Savannah entered the empty library. Principal Morgan was deep in conversation with Ms. Woodlawn behind the check-out counter. He wore his typical slacks, button-down oxford shirt, sweater vest, and bow tie. Add the heavy black frames of his glasses, and he was the epitome[112] of a nerd with the exception of

---

[106] Corroborate – strengthen or support with other evidence

[107] Artless – simple, natural

[108] Patently – openly, plainly

[109] Eschew – avoid, shun

[110] Exasperated – made very angry or annoyed

[111] Concur – to be of the same opinion, agree

[112] Epitome – a representative or example of a class or type

his linebacker physique.

Ms. Woodlawn's appearance was not as <u>meticulous</u>[113] as usual. A pencil <u>protruded</u>[114] haphazardly from her customary chignon, and her skirt and blouse were decidedly wrinkled and unkempt.

Neither of them had seen her enter.

"You know how I feel about this. And I don't think it's right to—" Ms. Woodlawn looked up to <u>espy</u>[115] Savannah <u>furtively</u>[116] ducking behind a rack of books. "Is that you, Miss Black?"

Savannah felt foolish. Her attempt to dart behind the book racks appeared suspicious. The principal and the librarian probably believed she'd been spying on them. "Um, I came in for a last minute cram session before Spanish next period." Although Savannah spoke the truth, it didn't sound so truthful when it came out of her mouth.

"I see." Ms. Woodlawn's skeptical tone created a pit of guilt in Savannah's stomach.

Principal Morgan straightened his already straight tie. "I guess I should be going. We'll talk about this matter later, Hetty."

"All right, Frank. But I don't think you can change my mind on this."

Principal Morgan formed a <u>peevish</u>[117] set to his mouth at that statement, but he <u>vacated</u>[118] the library without saying another word. When he passed Savannah he gave her a hard stare, which gave her the shivers. Principal Morgan had a <u>mercurial</u>[119] temper and could be intimidating when he wanted to be—bow tie or not.

Savannah slunk into a chair at one end of an empty table and immediately pulled out her Spanish book. She didn't want Ms. Woodlawn to suspect she came in there for any other reason than to study.

---

[113] Meticulous – extremely careful and precise

[114] Protruded – jutted out, projected

[115] Espy – catch sight of

[116] Furtively – in a shifty or stealthy manner

[117] Peevish – ill-tempered

[118] Vacated – moved out of, left

[119] Mercurial – quick and changeable in temperament, volatile

*

"You've made immense[120] progress since the last time I was here," said the voice in the dark.

Jenna had lost track of time. She wasn't sure how long she'd been in this black place. Her eyes must have adjusted to the dark, though, because she could make out shapes now. Her hoarse voice only allowed her to indicate yes or no in a series of grunts. She was also ravenous[121]. She'd never been so painfully, brutally hungry in her life.

She growled in anger, wishing her captor would finally bring her something besides water. A nice, juicy steak would taste sublime[122]. Or a cheeseburger. Her mouth watered at the thought. She tugged at the chain that held her there.

"I told you the hunger would grow, but it's necessary to preclude[123] you from eating. We have to wait until the time is right."

A knock sounded at the door.

"Come in," called out the voice.

The door opened, but this time no yellow light glowed. Jenna could see only the outline of a figure in the doorway.

This was something new. In the time Jenna had been in this place, the only contact she'd had with anyone else had been the voice. The voice brought her potable[124] water. The voice put an emollient[125] salve on her ankle where the shackle chafed. The voice talked to her about what life would be like after leaving this room.

Different. That is what she'd been told. Life would be different. She would see things differently. She would find herself changed in ways she couldn't imagine. She would want to emulate[126] and obey the Master.

After so much time in this one room with this one voice, Jenna grew accustomed to the fact something significant had

---

[120] Immense – extremely large, huge

[121] Ravenous – extremely hungry

[122] Sublime – not to be excelled, supreme, grand

[123] Preclude – to exclude or prevent from a condition or activity

[124] Potable – fit to drink

[125] Emollient – softening and soothing

[126] Emulate – strive to equal or excel, esp. through imitation

happened to her out in the woods that night. That didn't bother her. The fact she'd changed, the fact she would never truly be Jenna again wasn't abhorrent[127]. Her own personal thoughts and feelings had been pushed to the background. Other priorities filled her mind now.

Still, she had moments of paralyzing anger when she wanted to rage and claw things to pieces. Those were the hardest moments. Being shackled, she couldn't get any release from it. The anger, though, would soon become tractable[128], the voice told her. Something she could switch on and off as needed.

The figure in the doorway said, "It's time for her to go."

The door closed.

The comfort of the blackness returned. Jenna had grown used to the dark. She liked the dark now. Strange how one day something was her greatest fear and the next it became her greatest ally[129].

The voice spoke. "I'll unchain you now. You're free to go." Shuffling steps came her way. That strange, clawed hand touched her ankle. The clink of metal on metal echoed in the room, and then the shackle fell away.

Jenna's leg felt lighter than air. For some reason, when that hand ameliorated[130] her situation, her hunger instantly subsided[131] to a low purr in her stomach. She felt compliant[132] and relaxed, and in no hurry to leave her prison.

The door creaked open. A yellow rectangle of light blinded Jenna with its luminosity[133]. She put her hand up to her eyes to shield them. Her hand was no longer a hand. It, too, was a claw. Sharp nails like razor blades stuck out from the end of her fingertips. Long, brown hair covered the back of her hand.

This didn't surprise Jenna. She wasn't the same Jenna who found herself in this room however many days ago. She'd

---

[127] Abhorrent – disgusting, loathsome, or repellent

[128] Tractable – easily managed or controlled

[129] Ally – person connected with another in helpful association

[130] Ameliorated – made better

[131] Subsided – sunk to a lower or more normal level

[132] Compliant – submissive, yielding

[133] Luminosity – the quality of giving or radiating light

transformed into a new Jenna. A better Jenna.

She stepped toward the rectangle of light. As she approached the doorway, her claws receded. The long hair retracted[134] into her pale skin. Captivated[135], Jenna watched as her old hand reappeared.

"Yes, the light induces[136] the change to human form. That's how we're able to exist among the Others," elucidated[137] the voice behind her in the dark.

She turned to get a glimpse of the person who had soothed her and taken care of her needs during the fear and confusion of her captivity.

A shadowed figure moved toward her. A furry, clawed foot with the narrow width of a hind paw emerged from the darkness. After a few moments exposed to the light the foot transformed into a human foot. The figure took a few more steps into the light. In front of her stood a creature with a wolfish visage[138] , long fangs and low, pointed ears. Jenna felt no fear. She'd become the same as this creature now. A werewolf. Part human, part animal.

Slowly, in that warm yellow glow, the human manifested[139] itself. Ears receded into his skull, and the snout flattened into the planes of a face she could recognize.

"Jake," Jenna breathed. The light had changed her as well. Jake had been there all along, guiding her in her transformation.

Jake touched her shoulder. "The Master will come to you soon. All will be explained in time."

A question burned in her mind since the moment she awoke scared in the dark. "Did you choose me, Jake?"

"Yes."

She smiled at his answer. She was finally part of something bigger than herself. Although she'd lost part of Jenna in this room, she'd gained something far more valuable. She belonged.

---

[134] Retracted – drew back or in

[135] Captivated – attracted and held by charm, beauty or excellence

[136] Induces – brings about or stimulates the occurrence of

[137] Elucidated – made clear or plain

[138] Visage – face of a person, countenance

[139] Manifested – showed or demonstrated plainly, revealed

CHAPTER THREE

"You'll never guess who I just saw in fifth period." Dina accosted[140] Savannah in the crowded hall the next afternoon, earrings jangling. Dina and gossip were inextricable[141], and she appeared fit to burst with the news.

"A recruiter from Bryn Mawr who offered you a full-ride scholarship?" Savannah asked with a hint of sarcasm[142].

Dina jabbed her with her elbow, "No. Don't you ever have anything else on your mind than classes and college?"

"What else is there?" Savannah teased.

When Dina did her trademark eye roll, Savannah relented[143], "Okay, okay, tell me who you saw."

"Jenna Tinsley." Dina had a Cheshire grin on her face.

"Interesting."

So Jenna was back in school.

Savannah wanted to seek her out and ask her a few questions about her weekend. "Did she happen to mention where she was yesterday?"

"Nope. Mr. Peterson asked her for an excuse note, but Jenna ignored him."

"What did Mr. Peterson do?"

"Nothing."

---

[140] Accosted – approached and spoke to aggressively or boldly
[141] Inextricable – difficult or impossible to untangle or untie
[142] Sarcasm – a cutting, often ironic remark intended to wound
[143] Relented – became more lenient, compassionate or forgiving

Savannah's <u>disbelief</u>[144] must've been clear on her face.

Dina sighed. "Well, he marked something down next to her name. But he didn't send her to the principal's office or anything."

"Guess he was marking her down as an unexcused absence."

"But that's not the most important part." Dina stopped her in the hallway. Her voice lowered to a <u>conspiratorial</u>[145] murmur. "She was—different."

"Different?" Savannah asked in her regular speaking voice. What was all the hush-hush stuff about anyway? It wasn't as if they were discussing something illegal. Dina could be a little <u>melodramatic</u>[146] sometimes.

Dina loudly shushed her, <u>constraining</u>[147] Savannah from saying anything further. A few kids nearby them gave odd looks. Dina yanked her friend to a quiet corner near the stairwell.

"How was she different?" This time Savannah lowered her voice. She could play along with Dina's game. Her friend had <u>piqued</u>[148] Savannah's curiosity now.

"Her eyes. There was something about her eyes."

"Like what?"

"As if she could look right through me—through everyone. I've never seen her act like that before."

"What do you mean?"

Savannah caught a <u>glimpse</u>[149] of Jake Tanner sailing down the hallway, a gaggle of junior varsity football players swarming around him. "Look," she prodded Dina and pointed, "It's Jake!"

Dina raised her eyebrows and turned in the direction Savannah pointed.

As Jake passed by the stairwell, he turned his head their way. Savannah got caught up in his stare—his eyes glowed even in

---

[144] Disbelief – refusal or reluctance to believe

[145] Conspiratorial – in a secretive manner

[146] Melodramatic – exaggeratedly emotional or sentimental

[147] Constraining – inhibiting or restraining, holding back

[148] Piqued – provoked or aroused

[149] Glimpse – a brief, incomplete view or look

the well-lit hallway. Full of guile[150], they glittered like emeralds. Savannah's stomach roiled uneasily.

Did you see that?" Dina grabbed Savannah's arm. "His eyes—they were like Jenna's. It gives me the creeps."

"Yes, I saw them." A shiver ran through Savannah's body. She rescinded[151] any doubt she may have had about Dina's claims. She and Jenna shared a sixth period English class. It was exigent[152] that she get an answer straight from the horse's mouth.

*

"We don't have much time," growled the Master.

Jenna knelt before the powerful werewolf in the dimly lit room. She bent her head in submission[153] just as Jake had told her to present herself.

"Give me your arm."

Jenna rolled up the sleeve of her left arm.

"No, the other."

Jenna hesitated.

The Master struck her hard across the cheek.

Jenna flinched, discomfited[154] by the response to her mistake. She wanted to leap up, tackle the figure in front her, and make the Master pay for hurting her. But Jake had told her effrontery[155] would not be tolerated. The Master was the only one who could teach her the depths of her new abilities and the secrets of her kind.

"Do as I tell you," the Master intoned. "Now."

Not wanting to appear intractable[156], Jenna resolutely[157] rolled up her other sleeve and offered her arm to the Master.

A bell rang.

"We must hurry. There isn't much time."

The Master grabbed her arm, pulled it close, and twisted it

---

[150] Guile – treacherous cunning, skillful deceit
[151] Rescinded – made void, repealed, annulled
[152] Exigent – requiring immediate action or remedy
[153] Submission – yielding to the power or the authority of another
[154] Discomfited – made uneasy or perplexed
[155] Effrontery – brazen boldness, presumptuousness
[156] Intractable – difficult to manage or govern, stubborn
[157] Resolutely – firm or determined, unwavering

painfully. "I must give you the bite-mark, and then all will be clear to you." The black werewolf's powerful jaws were inches from Jenna's upper arm. In a flash, the fangs pricked her skin with a painful pressure.

The pain gave way to understanding. This was her Master. She would obey at all costs. A werewolf had powers beyond imagining, but those powers would only be used to protect the Master and do the Master's bidding. Images raced through Jenna's mind: claws sank into prey, eyes scanned the darkness to fathom[158] animals among the shadows, ears discerned the slightest noise in the brush. All these powers were now hers, but were only to be used in service to the Master.

The werewolf released Jenna, and she slumped back on her heels.

The bell rang twice.

"You must go now. Before you are missed," the Master ordered, like a despot[159] sending out his minions[160].

Jenna stumbled out of the darkened room. Her newly-sharpened vision caught every nuance[161] of color and light in the hallway. The ebb and flow of students through the building mesmerized[162] her for a moment.

Twenty yards away, at the other end of the hall, a voice caught her attention. Two girls near the stairs gossiped about her. She heard them as clear as a bell even at that distance. Jenna loved her new werewolf self. On the outside, in the daylight, she appeared to be a normal teenage girl. On the inside, however, powerful new talents emerged—more powerful than she could have imagined.

*

Savannah sat down in Mr. Reid's English Lit class. Since Jenna's desk stood a couple of rows behind hers, she didn't have a clear view of Jenna to confirm Dina's claims. After class Savannah decided to confront her about where Jenna had been for the past

---

158 Fathom – to penetrate and come to understand

159 Despot – a ruler with absolute power

160 Minions – a servile or fawning dependent

161 Nuance – a subtle or slight degree of difference

162 Mesmerized – hypnotized

few days. If Jenna was evasive[163], maybe Savannah could pry the truth out of her.

Savannah reflected on the memory of Jake's glowing eyes. They'd glowed even in the bright fluorescent lights of the hallway. How was that possible? Were her eyes playing tricks on her?

Jake had been missing from school for over a month. Why had she heard nothing about this on TV? Or at least something from the principal? Wouldn't Principal Morgan give the students an explanation why the captain of Northeast High's football team had been absent from the first few games of the season?

Rumors had run rampant[164] through school. At first, she'd heard Jake had been in a car accident and was on life support in the hospital. Then, the rumor morphed into a story about Jake's parents forcing him to attend a juvenile rehabilitation camp for out-of-control teens after he was arrested for vandalism. That rumor had been easily debunked[165]. Jake was popular and a bit of a jerk to the 'regular' students, but he wasn't the type to deface[166] an overpass with spray-painted graffiti. His most deleterious[167] acts included tripping kids in the hallway and sending fake love notes to a particularly nerdy kid. Nothing dangerous. Nothing that could be deemed illegal.

A rumble came from the back of the classroom. Class had started. Mr. Reid picked up a dry erase marker and covered the white board in passages from the book he'd assigned. The rumble heightened to a crescendo[168] of voices.

A girl who sat in the next aisle[169] poked Savannah. "Look, Jenna's back."

Mr. Reid stopped mid-sentence, turned, and looked down his glasses at his class. "I will not tolerate noise in my classroom."

The students quieted.

Savannah mimicked the rest of the class and turned to face

---

[163] Evasive – intentionally vague or ambiguous

[164] Rampant – occurring without restraint, unchecked

[165] Debunked – exposed or ridiculed the falseness or sham

[166] Deface – to mar or spoil the appearance or surface of

[167] Deleterious – having a harmful effect

[168] Crescendo – a steady increase in intensity or volume

[169] Aisle – a passageway between rows of seats

Jenna. Jenna perched in her seat, her back ramrod straight. Her blonde hair gleamed, her skin glowed, and her eyes were strange like Jake's. They glittered like sapphires. Savannah was drawn to their color and odd glow.

Mr. Reid rapped a ruler on the podium. Savannah jumped. Jenna blinked, breaking the tenuous[170] connection between them.

"Let's begin." The teacher opened a book. As he immersed[171] himself in reading from their assigned text, Savannah risked one more look over her shoulder at Jenna.

Jenna stared back.

Savannah shivered, but faked a smile.

Jenna slowly smiled back, but something insidious[172] lurked in that smile.

Savannah couldn't shake a timorous[173] feeling, as if she were a mouse in the presence of a very large cat.

"Ms. Black, could you answer the question for me?" Mr. Reid rapped on the podium for a second time.

Savannah whipped around. "I'm sorry, could you repeat it, please?"

"Please keep your eyes on the front of the class, Ms. Black."

Feeling abased[174], Savannah's face heated in peccancy[175]. She never grew distracted in class. Jenna's incredibly white smile, though, had made the hairs on the back of her neck stand up.

Jenna was definitely different. Jake, too. To get to the bottom of this mystery had become her new hobby. Savannah had to find a way to make Jenna disclose[176] exactly where she'd been last weekend. Maybe it was time to visit the Tinsley household once again.

*

"Why, hello. It's you again." Mrs. Tinsley answered the

---

[170] Tenuous – having little substance, flimsy

[171] Immersed – engaged wholly or deeply

[172] Insidious – intended to entrap, treacherous

[173] Timorous – full of apprehension

[174] Abased – lowered in position or estimation, degraded

[175] Peccancy – the state or condition of being sinful

[176] Disclose – make known

door.

Savannah had planned out a plausible[177] reason for stopping by. "Yes, I was hoping I could talk to Jenna."

"Oh?"

Savannah continued on wistfully[178], "Since I didn't go on the senior class trip, Jenna told me I could stop by to look at some of the pictures she took."

"Oh, sure." Mrs. Tinsley opened the door to let her in, "It's too bad you couldn't go along." Savannah heard genuine sympathy in Mrs. Tinsley's voice for the girl whose parents had ostracized[179] her from the senior class by not allowing her to go on the trip.

Savannah felt guilty deceiving Jenna's mother, but she needed to meet with Jenna. A closer inspection of Jenna would affirm if the changes Savannah perceived[180] in class were real or her imagination.

Savannah stood in a cavernous foyer. An elaborate[181], hand-carved staircase twisted elegantly up to the second story.

Mrs. Tinsley shut the door. "Jenna's room—"

"—is the first one on the left," finished Savannah.

"Oh, have you been here before?" Jenna's mother didn't remember their little study sessions from a few years' back. A wrinkle of confusion dented her smooth, alabaster forehead.

"It was a long time ago." Savannah hoped that might make Mrs. Tinsley feel better about forgetting her.

Savannah headed up the stairs. The floorboards creaked beneath her feet. Mrs. Tinsley disappeared inside the massive house.

The quiet unsettled[182] her. Once the tap of Mrs. Tinsley's high heels on the parquet floor faded away, the house grew unusually silent. Most teenage kids after school watched TV, listened to music, or hopped on the computer. Not a sound

---

[177] Plausible – seemingly or apparently valid, credible

[178] Wistfully – full of wishing yearning

[179] Ostracized – excluded from a group

[180] Perceived – became aware of directly through the senses

[181] Elaborate – intricate and rich in detail

[182] Unsettled - disturbed

emanated from the hall at the top of the stairs.

Jenna's door hung open a crack. Savannah vacillated[183] for a nanosecond.

"Come in, Savannah," Jenna called from within the darkened bedroom.

Goosebumps rose on Savannah's skin.

The door eased open. Jenna's eyes were luminous in the half-light.

"I was wondering when you would come." Her tongue flicked over her teeth. White, pointy teeth. Had her teeth always been so gleaming and sharp?

Savannah found it hard to pull her attention away from those teeth. She blinked. The connection broke. Savannah fought the urge to run. Her feet held her in place as if they were cement blocks.

"You can come in my room, if you want." Jenna opened the door further to give her admittance[184].

Why didn't Jenna's mother notice the difference in her own daughter? How could she miss the savage gleam in Jenna's eyes? Or the cold, preternatural[185] glitter of her sharp teeth even in the dimmest light?

Jenna exuded an animalistic, almost alien aura[186], as if the humanity had been sucked out of her. No warmth lingered here, only an emptiness. Savannah sensed it somewhere in the deepest part of her brain. As she stood mesmerized by Jenna's glittering eyes, the need to run overwhelmed her. She backed away from Jenna's room. She wanted to make a quick descent[187] down the steps but was afraid to turn her back on this new, unrecognizable Jenna.

"Don't go." Jenna took a step out of her room. "I'd like to talk to you."

---

[183] Vacillated – swung from one course of action to another

[184] Admittance – permission to enter

[185] Preternatural – out of or beyond the normal course of nature

[186] Aura – an invisible breath, emanation or radiation

[187] Descent – the act of moving or going downward

Savannah, her gait[188] erratic[189], tripped over her own feet to scramble down the stairs. Impelled[190] by instinct, she ran to the front door. She whipped it open and dashed to her waiting car. Anxiety pressed on Savannah's heart, and she fumbled with her keys. Jenna wasn't warm, wasn't real, wasn't human. At least, not anymore. Savannah knew she needed to get away and find Dina or Nick. They would listen to her.

She jammed the key into the ignition and started the car. When she looked up at the front porch of the Tinsley home Jenna stood inside the doorway, laughing, as if Savannah's perturbation[191] amused her.

Savannah's heart raced out of control. She gunned the engine and let her foot off the brake. Her car jumped forward and darted down the long driveway into the empty road. Her tires left behind long black skid marks.

Each mile she drove, her limbs relaxed a little and her heartbeat eased to a more even tempo. When she reached the middle of town Savannah pulled over into an empty parking space. Relief flooded her, and she slumped over the steering wheel.

Why did Jenna scare her so? What was it about her that made her seem so inhuman, so cold, so sinister? The black, icy grip of evil squeezed her heart the minute she'd approached Jenna's bedroom door.

Savannah had lived a prosaic[192] life up until this moment. She believed the good in humanity outweighed the bad. Life was a great adventure—a present waiting to be unwrapped. Today, those feelings of beneficence[193] and hope were stripped away. Jenna was no longer human. Something transpired[194] over the weekend. Jenna had been taken away and replaced with something else. Something atrocious[195].

---

[188] Gait – a particular way of moving on foot

[189] Erratic – having no fixed or regular course, wandering

[190] Impelled – driven forward, propelled

[191] Perturbation - agitation

[192] Prosaic – matter-of-fact, straightforward

[193] Beneficence – state or quality of being kind or charitable

[194] Transpired – happened or occurred

[195] Atrocious – extremely evil or cruel, monstrous

Savannah stared at her hands. They were pale and shaking, the veins a garish green against her skin. She was scared out of her wits. Jake's eyes glowed the same way as Jenna's. Whatever the two of them were, Savannah knew she couldn't let them infiltrate the school. They might pick off the students one by one—eating them or doing who knows what. They would be victims for whatever nefarious[196] purpose Jake and Jenna had in mind. The other burning question was, who or what had changed them?

Savannah had told her mother she'd be home in time for dinner. Although she wanted to drive straight to Dina's and tell her what had happened, she had to make it through dinner first. Later, she could sneak out her bedroom window and drive over to her best friend's house.

Savannah waited for the diminution[197] of her rapid breathing and drove slowly the rest of the way home. She focused on appearing as normal as possible. Walking into her house panting and wild-eyed would not be good idea. For a couple of hours she could play the normal kid at home. Then she could dump everything on Dina. Savannah drummed her fingers on the steering wheel. Her best friend had never let her down before. Savannah knew she wouldn't now.

---

[196] Nefarious – infamous by way of being extremely wicked
[197] Diminution – a lessening or reduction

CHAPTER FOUR

Jenna sat in a submissive position. The sticks and gravel on the forest floor ground into her hind paws, but she didn't flinch. Pain meant nothing to her anymore. Becoming a werewolf had expunged[198] her weakest human traits, such as sensitivity to pain.

The light of the waning[199] moon radiated[200] through the trees as it made a torpid[201] climb through the beautiful October night sky. Jenna caught the smell of burning leaves in the chilled night air. They weren't there, however, to appreciate the tranquility[202] of nature. Jenna, Jake, and Carter had obligations[203] to fulfill. Jenna must report her interaction[204] with Savannah.

"I was displeased with your behavior today among the humans." The Master stood tall in front of them. "You must not stand out. You must not appear as anything more than the humans you once were."

In the dark, they were all in their true form—claws sharp and at the ready, their metamorphosed[205] bodies covered in coarse

---

[198] Expunged – eliminated completely

[199] Waning – decreasing gradually in size, intensity, or degree

[200] Radiated – emitted light

[201] Torpid – slow

[202] Tranquility – a state of peace and quiet

[203] Obligations – the constraining power of a sense of duty

[204] Interaction – a mutual or reciprocal action

[205] Metamorphosed – changed wholly into a different form

fur. The werewolf form allowed the freedom to dash through the woods at night, leaping over downed trees and leaving swirls of colorful leaves behind. They had raced to the center of the woods as a pack. The sense of belonging was strong.

"But Master," Carter spoke up.

The head werewolf reached out fast as lightning to scratch Carter with sharp claws, drawing blood. The Master caught Carter in a chokehold and suspended him inches above the forest floor. The black werewolf stared into his eyes for a moment before dropping him with repugnance[206].

Carter clutched at his furry throat and sucked in air.

"You have much to learn, underlings[207]. We must be patient. For some of you, this may be a hard lesson to learn."

Carter backed away from the looming form in shame. Blood on his snout dripped to the ground.

"I need more recruits. On the next full moon, I will need more than one new addition to our clan." The Master nodded in Jenna's direction. "I expect you will choose with sagacity[208]?"

All three slave werewolves bowed their heads and nodded.

"You two brawny ones are good for protection" The black werewolf paced in front of them. "But I need perspicacity[209] as well. A trait you are both sincerely lacking."

Jenna crept forward. "May I speak freely?" Jenna knew compared to the two brutes next to her, she was clever and knew her place. Jake had intimated it had taken him weeks of training to learn about the transformation. Jenna caught on in less than a day. She was very adept[210].

The Master seemed pleased with the new slave. "You may."

"I know of three who may be useful to you. One of them already suspects."

"What? Someone knows your secret?" The Master growled in outrage and lifted a claw to strike.

---

[206] Repugnance – extreme dislike or aversion

[207] Underlings – of a lesser rank, subordinates

[208] Sagacity – quality of being sound in judgment, discerning

[209] Perspicacity – acuteness of perception or understanding

[210] Adept – very skilled

Jenna cowered, "No! She merely senses something is altered[211]. But she knows nothing."

"How can you be so sure?" The intimidating figure paced again.

"She was a friend once," Jenna said, impassive[212]. "I know her well."

"You think this friend would be a good asset?"

"She's more clever than I am."

A smile came over the Master's face. "You are a more useful neophyte[213] than I had hoped. We must have her."

"Yes, Master." Jenna bowed her head low.

"Yes, Master," Carter and Jake said in unison.

Clouds scudded across the moon and dampened the light to an anemic[214] glow. Four pairs of eyes glittered queerly in the dark. An owl hooted in the distance, the wind howled, and then the eyes were gone.

*

"You were right, Dina."

Savannah had climbed in Dina's bedroom window five minutes earlier. She was enthralled[215] her friend lived in a ranch-style house. Savannah was no athlete and even *thinking* about climbing a tree gave her palpitations. She didn't have the fortitude[216] for heights.

Dina sat amidst a pile of various drawings and doodles. How this girl managed to keep her 3.8 GPA was something Savannah never understood.

"I was?" Dina flipped through the pages of sketches and paused to look at a particularly well-drawn caricature[217] of Principal Morgan. She grinned.

"About Jenna." The harrowing[218] experience fresh in her

---

[211] Altered – changed, made different
[212] Impassive – revealing no emotion, expressionless
[213] Neophyte – beginner or novice
[214] Anemic – lacking vitality, listless, weak
[215] Enthralled – held spellbound, captivated
[216] Fortitude – strength of mind
[217] Caricature – picture with distorted natural characteristics
[218] Harrowing – extremely distressing, agonizing

mind, Savannah took a deep breath.

Dina dropped the paper in her hand. "What happened?" She swung her legs around and faced Savannah. She gripped her knees.

"I went to her house."

"You were in her house? Today?"

"Yes. You were right. There was something weird about her. Today in English Lit class, she had this look in her eye…"

Dina, <u>forbearance</u>[219] not her strong point, pressed her, "So, you went to her house and what happened?"

"Jenna's not Jenna. I mean, I don't know how to explain it, but she just isn't the same Jenna I knew last week."

"I don't understand. What do you mean? Like body snatchers or something?" Dina bit her lip. Her eyes lit up. "Maybe there are aliens in Centerville!"

Savannah tamped down the frustration building in her. "No, I'm not saying there are aliens or anything." She <u>expostulated</u>[220] the idea forming in her mind. "Something unnatural is going on. Like when the hair rises up on the back of your neck and you know something's wrong?"

"Yeah?"

"Well, that's how it was today at Jenna's house. I felt this evil presence in her. I had to get away from it."

"What kind of evil presence?"

"I don't know how to explain it. And her teeth…"

"Her teeth? This isn't the time to be talking about dental <u>hygiene</u>[221]," <u>chastised</u>[222] Dina.

"No, not that. I meant the way her teeth looked. There was something wrong about them. They were too…"

"Too what?"

"Too sharp." What Savannah wanted to say put her in a <u>quandary</u>[223]. The more she thought about what was wrong, the more she felt she was treading in the area of the supernatural. A 4.0

---

[219] Forbearance - patience

[220] Expostulated – discussed

[221] Hygiene – practices that serve to promote or preserve health

[222] Chastised – criticized severely, rebuked

[223] Quandary – a state of uncertainty or perplexity

student with a 2250 SAT score did not believe in the supernatural. It defied logic.

"What?" Dina's confusion was clear in her eyes.

"Forget it. I'm freaking out is all." Savannah thought it best not to rankle[224] her friend. She only speculated based on pure visceral[225] emotion. What she suggested was outlandish[226]. Another explanation must exist, and she wanted to research more before her friend shipped her off to the psychiatric ward.

"You don't just bring the words 'evil presence' into the conversation and then not explain yourself." Dina crossed her arms.

Savannah sighed. "I don't know what to tell you. I don't have any answers. I have no idea what's wrong with Jenna, but something clearly is."

"Okay, so what are we going to do about it?"

"*We?*"

"There's no way you're leaving me out of whatever kind of research you're going to do."

Dina knew Savannah too well. If something was inexplicable[227], Savannah always relied on books for an explanation. This situation was no different.

"We could start in the library tomorrow after school?" Savannah said tentatively[228]. Where in the heck did someone go for information on supernatural stuff? Tomes on the occult didn't appear from thin air. Northeast High's library was as good a place as any to start looking for answers. With internet access, too, Savannah wouldn't have to explain to her mother why she was online researching the occult[229] in the family living room.

"Library. After school." Dina scribbled furiously on a piece of sticky notepaper. "You got it. I'll make sure to let Nick know."

"Nick?" *Great.* Now Nick would think logical, reasonable

---

[224] Rankle – cause persistent irritation or resentment

[225] Visceral – felt as if in the gut

[226] Outlandish – bizarre, unconventional

[227] Inexplicable – difficult or impossible to explain

[228] Tentatively – uncertainly, hesitantly

[229] Occult –relating to or dealing with supernatural phenomena

Savannah was <u>demented</u>[230]. "I don't know."

"You don't *know*? He's our friend. We can't keep this from him. Besides, he might help us out."

Nick read at lightning speed. Dina was right. He could save them a lot of time. Plus, he was <u>proficient</u>[231] at science and a whiz on the computer. Maybe a scientific explanation for everything existed. If so, Nick would be the guy to find out.

"All right. Nick's in. But no one else."

"No one." Dina made an 'x' across her heart with her forefinger. "I promise."

Savannah fought the apprehension that bubbled in her heart. It wouldn't be so bad. There had to be an explanation for everything. Her two best friends in the world were going to help her find it.

So why did she feel so doomed?

---

[230] Demented – mentally ill, insane

[231] Proficient – having an advanced degree of competence

CHAPTER FIVE

The clock in the library read three-thirty. School had ended forty-five minutes ago, and Savannah saw no sign of Dina. She'd promised to meet her and Nick right after school.

Where was she?

Savannah and Nick sat at one of ten computers set up in the middle of the library. Dina had called up Nick last night to enlist[232] him in their research. Savannah found him willing, but a little baffled[233] about what was going on.

"So, now that I found this website on all things witchcraft[234], what do you want me to look for?" Nick sat back in his chair.

"Anything that fits what's been happening here at school."

"And what is that exactly? Kids who disappear and then reappear perfectly normal?"

"Not perfectly normal. Perfectly strange," Savannah maintained[235]. She wished he'd been at Jenna's house yesterday to see for himself. "Dina told you, Jenna was…well, she was…"

"Hey, guys." Dina strolled in as if everything were fine in the world. A pair of sparkly, imitation[236] diamond earrings swung back and forth from her earlobes.

---

[232] Enlist – engage the support or cooperation of
[233] Baffled – frustrated a person by confusing or perplexing
[234] Witchcraft – magic, sorcery
[235] Maintained – declared to be true, affirmed
[236] Imitation – something derived or copied from the original

"Where have you been?" Savannah asked petulantly[237].

"In the principal's office."

"What?" Nick pushed back from the computer. Shock reflected in his blue eyes.

"Why were you in Principal Morgan's office?" Savannah was as stupefied as Nick. "What happened?"

"I'm not in trouble or anything," Dina sat with a complacent[238] smile on her face. "I didn't tell you guys because if I didn't get picked, I didn't want anyone to know I even applied."

"Didn't get picked for what?" Savannah was more confused than ever.

"I applied to be the Homecoming Coordinator this year," Dina said with alacrity[239].

"What?" Nick and Savannah chorused.

"See? I knew you guys wouldn't understand."

Savannah was consternated[240] at the announcement. Her best friend didn't trust her enough to share her plans, and it hurt. "Understand what?"

"Why I wanted to do this."

"Well, you're right. We don't," Nick said tersely[241]. His expression darkened, and he returned to his online searching.

The three of them had been pretty close friends for the past couple of years. None of them were very popular. The job of Homecoming Coordinator usually fell to one of the girls in the popular crowd. Not Dina. Savannah viewed Dina's secrecy as perfidious[242]. Were they not good enough to be her friends anymore?

Dina pulled a thick folder labeled 'HOMECOMING' out of her backpack. "I thought you could at least be happy for me." She thumbed through pages of treasurer reports, contact information, and other vital Homecoming history in the folder.

---

[237] Petulantly – unreasonably irritable or ill-tempered

[238] Complacent – self-satisfied and unconcerned

[239] Alacrity – cheerful willingness or eagerness

[240] Consternated – to be in a state of paralyzing dismay

[241] Tersely – brief and to the point

[242] Perfidious – tending to betray, treacherous

"Sometimes I'm at the point of ennui[243] being one of the 'smart kids.' All we do is study, study, study. I wanted to try something different senior year."

Savannah sighed. Her indignation[244] at Dina's aspiration[245] to be popular was misplaced. The pulchritudinous[246] girls at school won over the gorgeous guys and had no worries about tests, grades, or SAT scores. She understood Dina's desire to break out of the geek mold. Dina had always been more interested in who was dating whom, what happened at some weekend bash near the lake, or who made out behind the bleachers after prom. Dina was smart, but she also longed to be a more social creature than Savannah or Nick.

"You're right, Dina. I'm sorry." Savannah touched her friend on the shoulder. "I'm happy for you. Actually, I'm amazed that Principal Morgan chose you instead of one of the cheerleaders. They're always in charge, and the theme ends up being something about puppies with a lot of pink streamers."

Nick spun around on his stool and beseeched[247] Dina, "Please tell me there will be no pink this year. Please."

Dina smiled at their interest in her new vocation[248]. "No pink. I promise."

"Then maybe I'll contemplate[249] going this year," Nick turned back to the computer. He missed the shocked looks on the girls' faces. Did that mean Nick had a date in mind for the Homecoming Dance?

Dina gave Savannah a quizzical look. Savannah shrugged her shoulders. If Nick had some secret crush, he hadn't let them in on it. At least, not yet.

"So, how did you get picked?" Savannah prompted.

"Principal Morgan asked me to apply."

---

243 Ennui – boredom

244 Indignation – anger aroused by something unjust or unworthy

245 Aspiration – an ambition

246 Pulchritudinous – having great physical beauty

247 Beseeched – addressed an earnest request to, implored

248 Vocation – occupation for which one is particularly suited

249 Contemplate – consider carefully and at length

"Really?" That was uncommon[250]. The principal typically cared very little for the social events on campus.

"Yeah. He called me to his office after school a couple of weeks ago and handed me the form. Said I would be the perfect person for this year's coordinator. Something about wanting to try a different tack this year." Dina pondered[251] for a minute. "Maybe he's sick of pink, too."

Savannah smiled, but in the back of her mind something didn't seem right. Why would Principal Morgan suddenly take an interest in the Homecoming dance? And why would he hand-pick Dina for the job of coordinator? She didn't think Principal Morgan even knew half the names of the kids in school, especially the estimable[252] kids with good grades. They usually stayed far off his radar.

Dina disrupted[253] her thoughts. "So, where do you want me to start the research?"

"Do you have time to help us?" Savannah focused her gaze at the protuberant[254] folder in front of Dina. It seemed fit to burst. "Homecoming's only three weeks away. Don't you have to start planning?"

"Are you looking for a reason to kick me to the curb?" Irritation filled Dina's voice. "I'm here. I'm willing. Put me to work, girlfriend."

Savannah was glad her friend's new responsibility wouldn't be a hindrance[255] to their friendship. "Yes, ma'am." She saluted Dina mockingly. "I pulled out the entire school library collection of books on the occult. I even threw in a few books on ESP and the paranormal just in case."

Dina eyed the small stack of books dubiously[256]. "This is it?" Less than ten books sat on the table between them.

"Yeah. Not too great, I know." Savannah tapped her pen

---

[250] Uncommon – not common, rare

[251] Pondering – weighing in the mind with thoroughness and care

[252] Estimable – deserving of esteem, admirable

[253] Disrupted – interrupted

[254] Protuberant – swelling outward, bulging

[255] Hindrance – something immaterial that interferes with action

[256] Dubiously – doubtful

on top of the book stack. "Guess the school's priority doesn't include adding the latest book on witchcraft into the library's collection. Nick's found some good stuff online, but there's so much information. It's going to be hard to weed through it all."

"Maybe we could ask Ms. Woodlawn for help. She might have some ideas." Nick lifted his chin in the librarian's direction. Savannah looked over her shoulder at the pristine[257] Ms. Woodlawn reshelving books in the reference section. Today she appeared more like her regular self—fastidiously[258] dressed, preened and perfect. Not a hair was out of place.

"Not a bad idea. Maybe there's something we could order from inter-library loan." Savannah tucked a notebook under her arm and headed to the back of the library. Ms. Woodlawn worked silently and slipped books into their appropriate spots on the shelves. Savannah's approach went unnoticed.

"Excuse me," peeped Savannah. Ms. Woodlawn, always so prim and neat, made her nervous. "I was hoping you could help us with some research."

Ms. Woodlawn slid a thick tome[259] onto a low shelf, and her reading glasses slid down her nose. "Research?" She perked up at that word. The librarian was very introspective[260] and not the type who would strike up a conversation with a student just to be friendly. She took her job very seriously.

"My friends and I are doing a paper on the supernatural."

"The supernatural?" Ms. Woodlawn brushed non-existent wrinkles out of her skirt and tucked imperceptible[261] wisps of hair into the discreet[262] bun on the back of her neck. She gave Savannah a penetrating[263] stare. "Which class would that be for?"

Savannah hadn't expected that question. She hesitated before answering, "It's an independent project, really. For a

---

[257] Pristine – remaining free from dirt or decay, clean

[258] Fastidiously – with meticulous attention to detail

[259] Tome – book, especially a large or scholarly one

[260] Introspective – examining own perceptual experiences

[261] Imperceptible – difficult to perceive by the mind or senses

[262] Discreet – free from ostentation or pretension, modest

[263] Penetrating – have the power of entering or piercing

scholarship." She extricated[264] that lie out of her brain somewhere.
"A scholarship?" Ms. Woodlawn echoed doubtfully.
"Yes." She prayed Ms. Woodlawn would believe her. If the librarian could facilitate[265] their search and find some useful resources, would it really matter if Ms. Woodlawn thought all three of them were nuts?

"I see." The librarian turned to her cart and selected another book to return to the shelves. She sniffed. "There may be a few books that I keep in storage. A little too obscure to put out on the regular shelves, you see. I suppose I could let you borrow them if you found something you could use."

Savannah smiled. "That would be great, Ms. Woodlawn. We'd really appreciate it."

Ms. Woodlawn added two slim volumes onto a shelf and beckoned Savannah to follow her behind the check-out counter. "I have a storage room back here. It's where I keep the new books that need to be catalogued and a few rarer items. Some were donations to the school, others—well, who knows where some of them came from." She pulled a key from a pocket in her skirt and unlocked a door half-hidden behind a fichus tree.

"This is great. Thanks so much."

"Promise me you won't take the books out of this building. You can look at them any time you'd like. Just ask." Ms. Woodlawn flipped a switch in the darkened room. A light illuminated[266] the small space. Innumerable[267] books were piled everywhere—some with thin slips of paper sticking out of them and others stacked in dusty piles. The scholar inside Savannah marveled at the hidden collection.

"Those have been catalogued." Ms. Woodlawn gestured at the books with the thin paper strips in them. "I just need to shelve them."

She and Savannah entered the room further. "And these are the books that might help you." She pointed at the

---

[264] Extricated – released from an entanglement, disengage
[265] Facilitate – make easy or easier
[266] Illuminated – provided or brightened with light
[267] Innumerable – to numerous to be counted

asymmetrical[268], dust-covered piles. "I think I recollect seeing one or two on the topic you mentioned. The librarian who preceded[269] me," she sniffed contemptuously[270], "had a predilection[271] for antique books. I've wanted to organize them for some time, but haven't had the opportunity."

"Great. Thanks." Savannah gave her a smile of gratitude. "This is really going to help out."

Ms. Woodlawn eyed her for a long moment. She sashayed past her. "Glad I could help. I'll leave this door unlocked while you're here."

Taking in the tall stack of books, Savannah sighed. This research stuff was going to take a lot longer than she thought.

*

An hour later Savannah sat on the floor of the storage room pouring over the eclectic[272] collection of books. At first, she found nothing useful. Most of the collection included abstruse[273] college textbooks some former Northeast student donated to his alma mater. A book covered in red-tooled leather, however, caught her eye.

The book, buried under manila folders and piles of papers, was unlike any other book in the room. The leather cover was embellished[274] in gold with swirls and cryptic designs. It had no title. When Savannah picked it up, the weight of it rested heavily in her hands.

Curious, she opened the book. Savannah turned each page gingerly as they were fragile and yellowed with age. The print had faded and some of the pages were missing, but the details within were incredible and endlessly fascinating. She relished[275] this kind of research. Her back ached, but she couldn't break away long enough to lug the book to the table. Nick and Dina were probably

---

[268] Asymmetrical – having no balance or symmetry, irregular

[269] Preceded – came, existed or occurred before in time

[270] Contemptuously - scornfully

[271] Predilection – preference, bias

[272] Eclectic – made up of different elements from many sources

[273] Abstruse – difficult to understand

[274] Embellished – made beautiful, decorated

[275] Relished – took a keen or zestful pleasure in

wondering where she'd disappeared to. They'd have to come find her.

The book held descriptions of <u>manifold</u>[276] supernatural beings, such as ghosts and druids. She finished reading a section on how to determine if a person had turned into a vampire, when Nick stepped into the room. "Hey, there, bookworm," he said in <u>salutation</u>[277]. "How's it going back here?"

Savannah eyed him from her spot on the hard tile floor. He really did have some amazingly blue eyes. Darn that Dina for pointing out how much Nick had changed! "Fine. I found a really interesting book."

"Interesting or useful?"

"I'm not sure yet. I haven't found anything about glowing eyes. There's no index, so it's going to take a long time to go through a book this big." She slipped her finger inside the book to hold her place, closed it, and showed him the thickness of it.

He sat down next to her. "I need a <u>respite</u>[278]. My eyes are about to fall out of my head. I've been sifting through webpages for almost two hours now." Nick nudged the book open. "Vampires, huh? I really want to believe you guys saw what you did. But vampires and witches? Doesn't that seem a little crazy?"

Savannah's heart sank. He doubted them. She <u>adhered</u>[279] to her story, however. "I don't know, Nick. If you'd been there. If you'd seen Jenna…" She couldn't explain any further. Her thoughts were <u>nebulous</u>[280] without a concrete theory to point to.

He sat cross-legged and rested his elbows on his knees. "I wish I'd been there. I don't like that you went there all by yourself," he <u>admonished</u>[281]. "It was <u>fortuitous</u>[282] that you got out of there okay. Until we know what's going on, we should stick together."

"Like the buddy system?"

"Yeah. I think we should promise each other we won't go

---

[276] Manifold – many and varied, multiple

[277] Salutation – a polite expression of greeting or goodwill

[278] Respite – short interval of rest or relief

[279] Adhered – remained devoted to, was in support of something

[280] Nebulous – lacking definite form or limits, vague

[281] Admonished – reproved gently but earnestly

[282] Fortuitous – lucky or fortunate

anywhere alone. I can drive you home after school."

"But then you drive the rest of the way home by yourself." Savannah pointed out.

"Okay. Then, how about any kind of investigating we promise to do together?"

A warmth spread through her insides at the suggestion. "I can agree to that."

Dina popped her head into the room. "Hey, guys. I have to get going. I do want to help out, but the Homecoming stuff…"

"We understand, Dina. It's okay." Savannah tapped Nick on the shoulder with her pen. "Nick and I decided to team up together. If we need any extra help, we'll let you know. Otherwise, don't worry about it." Little did Dina know Savannah's suggestion was self-serving. The idea of spending time alone with Nick sounded better and better. She hoped the dim lighting of the storage room hid her blush.

"If you find out anything, you'll let me know?" Dina's gaze shifted from Nick to Savannah.

Savannah nodded.

"Immediately?" Dina gave them both an <u>intent</u>[283] look.

"Of course," Nick assured her.

Savannah was glad he tried to <u>appease</u>[284] Dina's <u>anxiety</u>[285] over possibly being left out of the loop.

"Okay. If I notice anything else <u>suspicious</u>[286], I'll report back to you guys." Dina nodded her head. Her earrings jangled.

Nick got up and, with his usual <u>geniality</u>[287], reached out his hand to Savannah to help her up.

"Sounds like a deal." Savannah accepted Nick's assistance and hoped her hands weren't clammy. Did she detect a glint of warmth in Nick's gaze when their hands touched? Her stomach fluttered at the thought.

Before leaving the storage room, she grabbed a piece of notebook paper and tucked it into the book to mark her place. She

---

[283] Intent – firmly fixed, concentrated
[284] Appease – bring peace, quiet, calm to; soothe
[285] Anxiety – state of uneasiness and apprehension
[286] Suspicious – arousing suspicion, questionable
[287] Geniality – having a friendly disposition or manner

didn't want to relinquish[288] it and wished she could take it home with her. Savannah had the urge to purloin[289] it, but had no way to hide such a large book. If she *did* have the guts to swipe the book, it would likely distract her from her homework. Savannah didn't want to risk her grades slipping. Weird things might be happening at Northeast High, but she needed to keep her eye on graduation. She hoped Ms. Woodlawn would live up to her promise and let her back into the storage room another day.

Reluctantly[290], she placed the tome on top of the dusty heap of books in the corner. Its red leather and gold embossed cover stood out from the clutter of paperbacks and reference materials heaped in the small room. When she got a chance to get back in the storage room, that book should be easy to find.

Only one thing was clear to her that afternoon: They weren't dealing with vampires. Vampires couldn't be out and about in the daylight. How ridiculous to even be thinking about vampires. However, the book would provide empirical[291] data to eliminate the possibilities until they found an answer. The situation was analogous[292] to any experiment she might conduct in physics class.

Positive the book held answers, Savannah looked forward to tomorrow afternoon when she could continue her research.

"You coming?" Nick stood in the doorway.

"Yeah. I'll be with you in a sec." She begrudgingly[293] left the book behind. That book was integral[294] to their research, and she was loath[295] to leave it. What choice did she have?

On her way out, she wanted to find Ms. Woodlawn and let her know she could lock up the storage room. The librarian was nowhere to be seen. Savannah thought nothing of leaving the library, positive Ms. Woodlawn would lock up the room when she left for the evening.

---

[288] Relinquish – cease holding physically, release

[289] Purloin - steal

[290] Reluctantly – unwillingly

[291] Empirical – derived from observation or experiment

[292] Analogous – similar in some respects but otherwise dissimilar

[293] Begrudgingly – reluctantly

[294] Integral – essential or necessary for completeness

[295] Loath – unwilling, reluctant

CHAPTER SIX

Jenna was hungry.

A week had passed since her transformation, and the insatiable[296] hunger returned. Jake told her it would. This hunger was different than the hunger she had once known as a human. Werewolf hunger demanded attention. Sudden and painful, it pounced on her at the most inopportune[297] time. Today, it grabbed hold of her during second period gym class while she waited for a drink of water.

Her corpulent[298] gym teacher had organized volleyball matches between the girls' class and the boys'. The girls sat bored on the bleachers in the gym as they waited for teams to be picked. Thirsty, Jenna headed to the drinking fountain at the far end of the gym. The terrible pangs struck like a jolt of electricity. She groaned and doubled over from the sudden onset[299] of hunger.

"Are you okay?" A chubby brunette had finished her drink at the fountain.

The scent of the girl overwhelmed her nostrils. Fresh blood coursed through the body in front of her. A body Jenna salivated to devour right there in the gym in front of everyone.

Jenna had to be pragmatic[300]. She had to wait for the right

---

[296] Insatiable – impossible to satisfy

[297] Inopportune – inappropriate or ill-timed

[298] Corpulent – excessively fat

[299] Onset – a beginning, a start

[300] Pragmatic – dealing or concerned with facts, practical

opportunity to strike. She craved[301] human flesh the most, but almost any fresh meat would do. Lots of people would miss this girl if Jenna chose her as her first meal. Although tempting[302], the warm body wasn't tempting enough to disobey the Master. The black werewolf had warned them to better mask themselves among the humans. No one must suspect they had changed or the Master's plans would be impeded[303].

Guarding and keeping the Master concealed from everyone ranked as the first and most important order for the slave werewolves. Selecting new recruits[304] and initiating[305] them into the pack ranked the second most important. Jenna's discomforts[306] and wants landed at the bottom of the list. Controlling her hunger was her responsibility.

She swallowed the saliva threatening to drip out of her mouth. Tonight she would hunt. Tonight she would feed on something more suitable than the fat, fleshy girl in front of her. A dog perhaps.

"Girls!" The gym teacher blew her whistle and called her class back to the center of the floor.

The chubby girl wiped her mouth with the back of her pudgy arm, smiled, and jogged off to the group. Jenna took a quick lap of the cold water and forced down her desire to eat. She trotted back to her class.

"Let's start picking teams. We only have thirty-five minutes until the end of the period." The teacher glanced at her watch.

Jenna focused her thoughts on appearing as human as possible by downplaying her enhanced[307] reflexes and dulling her vision. If she concentrated hard enough, the glow in her eyes was barely perceptible.

"Jenna, you'll be a team captain. And Grace." The teacher

---

[301] Craved – had an intense desire for

[302] Tempting – having strong appeal, enticing

[303] Impeded – retarded or obstructed the progress of

[304] Recruit – a new member of an organization or body

[305] Initiating – admitting into membership with a ritual

[306] Discomforts – mental or bodily distress

[307] Enhanced – increased or intensified in value or quality

pointed at a petite girl with black hair.

When Jenna's turn came, she couldn't help it. She picked the chubby girl for her team. Even if Jenna couldn't devour that succulent[308] flesh, she could fantasize, couldn't she?

*

Jake sat in chemistry class, and his eyes drooped. He had hunted late the night before, and this morning he was somnolent[309].

"Mr. Tanner? Are you with us today?" His chemistry teacher, Mr. Boyd, tapped on Jake's desk with his ubiquitous[310] pointer. He never taught a class without it.

Jake snapped awake. He fought the impulse to leap on the man in front of him and tear him to pieces.

Mr. Boyd took a step back. For a moment, Jake had lost control. He knew his teacher saw the uncanny[311] glow of his eyes. Jake blinked and reined in his inner werewolf.

"Those darn fluorescent bulbs make everything look funny," Mr. Boyd muttered. Mr. Boyd cleared his throat and continued with the lesson covering the bonds between electrons.

Jake slid down further. His long legs stuck out into the aisle. He closed his eyes to slits. If he could just catch a few minutes of sleep, he would feel better. Tonight he wouldn't have to feed. Tonight he could sleep.

*

The Master monitored the next candidate selected for transformation. Observation[312] had been continuous[313] since the slaves chose this girl. The Master approved of their choice—bright, yet quiet and respectful. That's what the Master needed. No more of these brutes with their boorish[314] ways and scurrilous[315] behavior. An intelligent slave would be worth much more.

---

[308] Succulent – juicy or delectable
[309] Somnolent – drowsy, sleepy
[310] Ubiquitous – ever present
[311] Uncanny – peculiarly unsettling, eerie
[312] Observation – the act of watching
[313] Continuous – uninterrupted in time, substance or extent
[314] Boorish – rude
[315] Scurrilous – grossly indecent or vulgar

Plans for the ultimate[316] defense would begin once her transformation was complete. One needed soldiers to carry out orders without question, but one also needed an officer to plan and organize. An intelligent officer could handle the job much better than those two buffoons—Jake and Carter.

Three weeks remained before the next full moon. Transformation must be carried out at midnight on the night of the full moon. The boy would coax her into the woods for the ceremony, and the girl slave would help.

Now they must find a way to get close to her, befriend her, and bring her into their confidence[317]. The girl suspected something was strange about them, which created difficulties. These difficulties, however, made her transformation even more imperative[318]. A possible enemy would be turned into an asset.

What a coup that would be.

The girl slave, Jenna, mentioned the candidate had friends who had their suspicions. Change one, and they could change them all. A Master needed a host of intelligent slaves to stay alive. The risk would be worth it in the end.

The werewolf refused to be weak again. No one would ever supplant[319] the Master. No one would ever defeat the Master. Not with the slaves the black werewolf gathered. A strong band of loyal slaves would assure safety and secrecy.

A memory flitted through the Master's mind—a time of weakness and fear long before the transformation. For a short moment, the large, black werewolf was a child cowering[320] in a closet, waiting for the hard strikes that were sure to come. A cold sweat broke out on the Master's forehead. Only anger, pain, and fear remained in that memory.

The Master's hands curled into themselves. Claws drew blood from the palms. The Master snarled at the memories of weakness and vulnerability[321] that rushed back.

---

[316] Ultimate – beyond which there is nothing else

[317] Confidence – that which is confided, a secret

[318] Imperative – urgent, pressing

[319] Supplant – to take the place of, especially through intrigue

[320] Cowering – cringing in fear

[321] Vulnerability – susceptible to physical or emotional injury

"Master?" A figure appeared in the crack of the door.
"What is it?"

The slave boy, Carter, trembled. "I think we have an opportunity[322]."

The slave's fearful demeanor[323] caused the Master pleasure. "Is that so?"

"Yes, we're all joining the Homecoming Committee."

Gratification[324] shattered the Master's fearful memories. "You'll make sure not to frighten her any longer?"

"We'll appear as we used to be. We've been practicing. Jenna is really good at masking the changes, and she's teaching us the same methods."

"Yes, let her instruct you. She's a fast learner."

"Yes, Master."

Jenna had been a most excellent choice. Idiot slave, Jake, had done only one thing right since his transformation—choose Jenna as a candidate. He redeemed[325] himself a little bit at a time for that choice.

"Be sure to move slowly. We don't want to frighten such a promising recruit. You must first prove her suspicions wrong before she will trust you."

"Yes, Master."

A bell rang in the distance.

"We both must go. Away with you." The Master enjoined[326] him and flicked sharp claws in Carter's direction, urging him to leave quickly.

He took the hint and slipped away out the door and down the corridor beneath the school.

This sepulcher[327] of a hiding place wouldn't be useful much longer. A larger slave clan would need a bigger place to hide. A storeroom in the labyrinth[328] of the school basement would only

---

[322] Opportunity – a chance for progress or advancement

[323] Demeanor – the way in which a person behaves

[324] Gratification – satisfaction

[325] Redeem – restore the honor, worth or reputation of

[326] Enjoined – directed or imposed with authority and emphasis

[327] Sepulcher – a burial vault

[328] Labyrinth – maze

hold so many. A new lair must be found soon. At least one more would join them. If the girl slave had the <u>acumen</u>[329] as suspected, maybe even three new recruits would join their ranks.

The Master smiled at the prospect. Safety would be certain with a clan as large as that. A <u>shrewd</u>[330], intelligent clan guaranteed the Master would stay alive.

---

[329] Acumen – quickness and keenness of judgment or insight
[330] Shrewd – sharp intelligence, keen awareness

CHAPTER SEVEN

Dina waited in the empty classroom after school. Her inchoate[331] Homecoming Committee meeting began in a matter of minutes. She needed a good group of kids to help with all the planning. Rather than be quixotic[332], she knew her lack of popularity might detract from recruiting the typical volunteers—cheerleaders and jocks.

A few varsity cheerleaders walked in and alleviated[333] her fears. She smiled and shuffled the papers in front of her. Dina had stacked sign-up sheets, schedules and a list of theme ideas on the podium, which awaited debate[334]. Although she wanted a committee to make most of the decisions, she wasn't above reducing the choices to focus on the ones she thought were best. She hoped that went over well with the popular crowd.

At five minutes after three, volunteers packed the room. Excitement filled Dina at her success attracting so many students. Perhaps her level of popularity had nothing to do with it. She cleared her throat to begin the meeting. The room quieted.

Jenna, Jake, and Carter strolled in.

Dina was stupefied[335] to see them. The trio took seats near the back of the room. Though inside Dina was wary of these new

---

[331] Inchoate – in an initial or early stage, incipient

[332] Quixotic – idealistic without regard to practicality

[333] Alleviated – made easier to bear, relieved

[334] Debate – deliberation, consideration

[335] Stupefied – amazed, astonished

arrivals, outside she put on a veneer[336] of cool friendliness. She knew her suspicions about these three had yet to be proven true.

Dina had to admit that since the one encounter with Jenna and her frightful[337] glowing eyes, she had yet to see a repeat performance. More odd was the fact Jenna had hung out every day that week with Jake and Carter. Before last weekend, Dina wasn't sure Jenna even knew those boys.

The varsity cheerleaders, who'd entered the room first, eyed Jenna suspiciously. This new triumvirate[338] threw them off balance. What was a member of the Chess Club and known smart person doing with two of the hottest guys in school? The cheerleaders hid their rancor[339] and reluctantly embraced her presence, probably because they wanted to stay close to Jake and Carter. Perhaps they believed the football jocks would get sick of Little Miss Smarty Pants and come back to their senses.

Dina cleared her throat again to get the meeting started. The cheerleaders might begin to think she couldn't handle the responsibility usually given to one of them. "Welcome to the Homecoming Committee meeting. I'm glad to see all of you here. If we want to have an awesome Homecoming Dance this year, I'm going to need all of your help."

Dina grabbed their attention and held it for all sixty minutes of the meeting. They approved her theme ideas and schedule without much discussion. Surprisingly, the group of popular people had very little to complain about. Dina was proud she'd managed to do a stellar[340] job of guiding the ideas in the direction she wanted.

No pink. No puppies or kittens. Nick would give her accolades[341] for that.

The meeting came to a close with committees organized and projects assigned. The obstreperous[342] group of cheerleaders

---

[336] Veneer – a deceptive, superficial show

[337] Frightful – causing disgust or shock, horrifying

[338] Triumvirate – an association or group of three

[339] Rancor – bitter, long-lasting resentment

[340] Stellar - outstanding

[341] Accolades – expressions of approval, praise

[342] Obstreperous – aggressively boisterous

and jocks filed out of the room. When the last cheerleader left, Dina reached for the light switch. A familiar voice stopped her.

"Dina?" Jenna stood in a far corner of the room.

Dina's gaze riveted on the slim blonde. She quelled a feeling of unease that grew inside her. Nothing ominous[343] had happened during the meeting. In fact, Jenna suggested a few good ideas for the dance decorations. Dina hovered near the door, adverse[344] to being too close to Jenna. She remembered very clearly that day in class when Jenna's eyes held a strange intensity.

"Yes?" She fiddled with one of her dangling earrings. Where did Jake and Carter go?

"I was wondering if I could help you buy some of the supplies when the time comes." Jenna's voice had a conciliatory[345] lilt.

Relief flooded Dina with her simple request. "Oh. Sure. That'd be great to have some help." Jenna wanted to be accommodating[346]. Nothing strange about that. Come to think of it, nothing strange about Jenna's eyes today. She appeared to be perfectly normal. More fashionable than usual, but normal nonetheless.

"Great." Jenna flashed a quick smile. "Let me know when, okay?"

"Sure. Probably a few days before the dance."

"Okay." Jenna gave her a friendly wave before she headed down the hall.

Dina was mystified[347]. Had her instincts been off the other day? Jenna was disparate[348] from the person she'd been a few days ago. Not the old Jenna, but neither was she the scary, malevolent Jenna who had been in her class the other day. Was there some legerdemain[349] going on? Or had she and Savannah been horridly off-base with their suspicions?

---

[343] Ominous – menacing, threatening

[344] Adverse – contrary to one's interests or welfare

[345] Conciliatory – tending to reconcile

[346] Accommodating – helpful, obliging

[347] Mystified – confused or mentally puzzled

[348] Disparate – fundamentally different, entirely dissimilar

[349] Legerdemain – deceitful cleverness, sleight of hand

She *could* use the help with the supplies. Unless someone else on the committee stepped up to help with the shopping, Dina was tempted to accept Jenna's offer. Dina checked to make sure she had all the sign-up sheets tucked away in the folder she'd set aside for her Homecoming Coordinator position. She took the job seriously and wanted no less than the best Homecoming Dance of her high school career.

*

Savannah sighed. Her essay for her application to Brown wouldn't write itself. She rested her chin in her hand and gazed across the library. One, lone freshman sat at the bank of computers. Most students deserted the library by three-thirty in the afternoon. Even Ms. Woodlawn disappeared into a back room after Savannah arrived.

Their supernatural research had ended abruptly[350] last Friday. Nick, tired from slogging through thousands of web hits on every topic from angels to tropical diseases, begged off another afternoon of fruitless searching. Sure, that interesting book in the storage room had looked promising. However, Savannah had begun to think it was ridiculous[351] to spend so much time looking for a reason why high school students might have glowing eyes and personality changes. She had homework to do, essays to write and a valedictorianship to attain[352]. These things took time and a lot of mental energy. With Dina engrossed[353] in planning the Homecoming Dance, Savannah's enthusiasm[354] for the project waned. Besides, since that one day at school, Savannah had witnessed no more strange behavior. Jenna's eyes appeared fever-bright from time to time, but they didn't hold the same eerie glow they had during English Lit class.

Maybe they should give up. Her fears from that afternoon at Jenna's house could've been her imagination. If that were true, then she felt completely stupid for her egregious[355] behavior.

---

[350] Abruptly – unexpectedly sudden
[351] Ridiculous – silly, foolish
[352] Attain – achieve, gain as an objective
[353] Engrossed – occupy exclusively, absorbed
[354] Enthusiasm – great excitement or interest
[355] Egregious – conspicuously bad or offensive

Running from Jenna's house because she had extra pointy teeth? It must be all in her head, right? Jenna must think she was an abject[356] idiot. No wonder Jenna avoided her as of late in the hallways.

"Ms. Black?"

Savannah snapped out of her daydream and focused her gaze on Principal Morgan who hovered over her. Instantly[357], she straightened her back to appear more studious[358].

"Hi, Principal Morgan." This was unusual. The only time she talked to the man was when she received some award at the end of the school year. Otherwise, they crossed paths only occasionally in the main office when Savannah met with her school counselor.

"May I talk to you for a moment?" The acerbic[359] quality in his voice put Savannah on alert.

The library had emptied. The freshman at the computer had disappeared. A twinge[360] of nervousness gripped her stomach. Her hands grew clammy. She rubbed the cold sweat on her jeans. "Sure."

Why would he need to talk to her?

The clock on the wall read four o'clock. Where did Ms. Woodlawn go? Savannah wished with all her might the librarian would walk into the room at that very moment.

"I would prefer it if we talked in my office." Principal Morgan rolled back his shoulders as if he were loosening up for a fight.

Bowtie or not, Principal Morgan was intimidating[361]. He had an amplitudinous[362] figure, which blocked the ultra-bright fluorescent light. Savannah slumped under the shadow. "All right."

She gathered her papers and books and stuffed them into her backpack. Savannah was flabbergasted[363]. Why would he want

---

[356] Abject – of the most contemptible kind
[357] Instantly – at once
[358] Studious – given to diligent study
[359] Acerbic – sharp or biting, as in character or expression
[360] Twinge – a sudden, sharp feeling
[361] Intimidating – discouraging through fear
[362] Amplitudinous – of large proportions
[363] Flabbergasted – astounded, surprised

to see her? What would he possibly need to tell to her?

"I've been meaning to talk to you for awhile" Principal Morgan led her down the hall toward the main office. His thin mouth was set in a determined[364] line.

"Oh?" Savannah was equivocal[365] that this was a benign[366] conversation.

He held open one side of the double glass doors that led to the receptionist's desk and his office beyond.

"Yes, last week. You overheard a conversation I was having with Ms. Woodlawn."

They entered his cramped, windowless office.

"I don't remember," Savannah prevaricated[367]. What had she overhead that was so terrible? From her recollection it had been nothing more than a minor disagreement.

"Well, I do." Principal Morgan sat behind his undersized metal desk. Nothing but the best for a public school principal. "I want you to understand there are things that go on behind the scenes at Northeast High that have nothing to do with the student population."

Savannah settled into a highly uncomfortable chair. By the austere[368] look on Principal Morgan's face, she was to be seen and not heard during this particular discussion.

"Teachers and administrators have responsibilities that far surpass those you are aware of. The school is part of the community, and we do our best to…"

Savannah couldn't bear to hear anymore, "Sir, I really didn't hear a thing between you and Ms. Woodlawn. Not more than a sentence or two. Honestly." She had no idea why he needed to bring her into his office for a full-blown lecture. What exactly had that conversation been about anyway? Had she done or said anything in the past week to indicate she knew something she shouldn't?

Principal Morgan closed his mouth. He gave her a

---

[364] Determined – decided or resolved

[365] Equivocal – of a doubtful or uncertain nature

[366] Benign - harmless

[367] Prevaricated – strayed from or evaded the truth

[368] Austere – severe or stern in disposition or appearance

scathing[369] glare and pulled open a desk drawer. "Then why did I procure[370] *this* from inside your locker today?" He whipped out a black notebook with a flourish, as if its existence alone implicated[371] her in some sordid[372] scheme.

"My locker?" Savannah was dumbfounded. The principal had been snooping in her locker?

"Yes." Principal Morgan brandished the notebook. "When I saw you in the library I was suspicious you may have heard some compromising information. When I saw you in the storage room, I knew."

"Knew what?" Savannah challenged. "That I'm doing research for a scholarship?" The notebook held notes she'd taken about their investigation[373] into the Jenna mystery.

"Research on the occult?" he asked skeptically. He flipped to the first few pages in her notebook, where she had sketched out a pentagram[374] and some other symbols.

"Look, Principal Morgan, I'm not quite sure how my research has anything to do with some conversation you had with the librarian. Really, I don't." She knew her words were defiant[375]. She clutched her backpack as if it would afford her some sort of protection. "I'd like my notebook back, please." She held out her hand, waiting. Principal Morgan scared her. He'd always been a staid[376] and stolid[377] man, but she wasn't about to back down from her demand. It was a notebook, for gosh sake's, with notes about witches and paranormal events.

He gave her a redoubtable[378] glare, as if he were studying her under a microscope and looking for a way under her skin. He wanted something from her, but she wasn't quite sure what. After a

---

[369] Scathing – sharp, critical, hurtful

[370] Procure – get by special effort, acquire

[371] Implicated – involved or connected intimately

[372] Sordid – of degraded character or nature

[373] Investigation – detailed inquiry or systematic examination

[374] Pentagram – a star with five points

[375] Defiant – bold opposition, challenging

[376] Staid – of a steady and sober character

[377] Stolid – having or revealing little emotion or sensibility

[378] Redoubtable – arousing fear or awe, formidable

few long, tense moments, he handed her the notebook.

She slipped it into her backpack. "Can I go now? I have a lot of studying to do." She hid her trembling hands from him, so he wouldn't know how much he'd frightened her.

"Just stay out of that storage room. That's no place for you," he growled.

"But Ms. Woodlawn…"

"Ms. Woodlawn does not run the school."

"Yes, sir." Savannah's momentary[379] courage quickly dispersed[380].

"Whatever kind of research you need to do, perhaps it would be better if you went to the public library. They have better resources anyway."

"Yes, sir." She wanted to get out of the stifling[381] room as soon as possible.

"I'd better not see you in here again, Ms. Black." Principal Morgan wagged a threatening finger at her. "Remember, I'm keeping an eye on you."

Savannah shut the door solidly behind her. What was that all about? Why wouldn't he want her in that storage room?

An idea hit her like a bolt of lightning. Could it be that Principal Morgan was involved in the mystery? Was he the one who abducted[382] Jenna and the two boys and turned them into something else? Something inhuman?

For the past several days it everything had returned to normal. No weird glowing eyes. Nothing scary or strange. But why would the principal be so adamant[383] about her staying out of the storage room? Why was he so interested in what was in her notebook? The only answer that made any sense was that he was involved. She and Nick were getting close to the truth. That *had* to be it.

Shivers ran down her back. The office had emptied. Even the school receptionist, who usually stayed until five o'clock, had

---

[379] Momentary – lasting only for a moment

[380] Dispersed – broke up, vanished

[381] Stifling – to the point of being almost suffocating

[382] Abducted – carried off by force, kidnaped

[383] Adamant – stubbornly unyielding

left. Savannah exited into the empty hallway and took long strides to get to her car as fast as possible.

She turned over this new possibility in her mind. If Principal Morgan was involved and worried about what her notebook might reveal, she had to get back inside that storage room. There must be something in there he didn't want her to see. Something in that old red book perhaps? She wasn't going to abort[384] their research now.

First, she had to let things cool down a bit before she attempted to acquire[385] access to that room. Hopefully, the principal hadn't spoken to Ms. Woodlawn yet. She resolved[386] to come early in the morning, before school. The library opened at 7:30. It was worth a try. Ms. Woodlawn might scold her for going against the principal's edict[387], but she was willing to take that risk.

Only a few cars were parked in the lot. Realizing the principal might be involved in something dark, Savannah rushed to unlock her car. She'd be a sitting duck if the principal changed his mind. Her car key slipped easily into the lock.

Calm down, Savannah. It's broad daylight. The football team is practicing right over there.

She remained vigilant[388]. The football field lay a hundred yards away. If something happened they would certainly hear her scream. Besides, if Principal Morgan had wanted to do something to her, why would he have let her leave his office? He must have known a myriad[389] of people were around to witness any action against her.

Still, she didn't feel safe until she drove several miles from school. She felt even better when she pulled her Corolla into Nick's driveway. Savannah wasn't going to keep this suspicion to herself. Since Dina would be swamped with Homecoming activities, Nick would be her best option.

---

[384] Abort – terminate an operation or procedure before completion
[385] Acquire – come into possession of something
[386] Resolved – made a firm decision about
[387] Edict – a formal pronouncement or command
[388] Vigilant – on the alert, watchful
[389] Myriad – constituting a very large, indefinite number

CHAPTER EIGHT

"You think Principal Morgan is involved?" Nick shared a bowl of freshly popped popcorn with Savannah.

They were pretending to watch a movie in his living room. Nick's mother, elated he'd brought home a female friend, had shooed away Nick's younger brother. Nick reddened at what his mother's actions implied[390]. Savannah's worries, though, allowed him to repress[391] any embarrassment.

"It makes sense, doesn't it?" Savannah grabbed a handful of popcorn. "It explains why he didn't seem concerned about anyone missing and why he wouldn't answer questions at the PTA meeting." She hoped Nick would assess[392] the facts and come to the same determination[393].

"I guess so." Nick's expression clouded over. "But he's been the principal at Northeast for, like, twenty years. Why would he kidnap students? It doesn't make a whole lot of sense."

She drummed a finger on her can of soda. "Then why would he have searched my locker? Why would he be so concerned about my notebook? I think he's worried we may have stumbled onto something."

Nick mulled over her suspicions and reclined[394] comfortably

---

[390] Implied – expressed or indicated indirectly

[391] Repress – put down by force

[392] Assess – determine the value, significance, or extent of

[393] Determination – the act of making or arriving at a decision

[394] Reclined – lay back

on the couch. "That's true. It doesn't make much sense. I wonder what he thinks you overheard in the library? If he's hiding something, why would he be talking to Ms. Woodlawn about it?"

"I don't know. That's one piece of the puzzle that doesn't quite fit." That thought encumbered[395] her. How was Ms. Woodlawn involved in all this?

"Principal Morgan pulling you into his office means we must be close to the truth. What do you think he's hiding in that storage room? Something evidential[396]?"

"This isn't a criminal case we're talking about, Nick. It's something even our own parents wouldn't believe if we told them. I mean, come on, supernatural occurrences? Maybe demonic possession[397]?"

"But if that's the case, why did you and I both decide we were wrong?" he reminded her. "Jenna seemed pretty much back to normal."

"I'll concede[398] she doesn't have those creepy eyes anymore. At least, not that I've noticed. But I still can't shake the feeling I had in her house that day. I wanted to believe it was nothing, but now that I think more about it…"

"We gotta get back in that storage room, don't we?" Nick reached for the TV remote and lowered the volume. Their discussion had grown more and more clamorous[399] to compete with the blaring movie soundtrack.

"Yep." The sound of her own voice seemed unnaturally loud, so she modulated[400] it a bit. "I think that's the only way we're going to make any headway."

"So, what's the plan?"

"Tomorrow, we're going to sneak in there before school starts. We'll concoct[401] some story so Ms. Woodlawn lets us in that room one more time. Now that we know something important is

---

[395] Encumbered - burdened

[396] Evidential – of, providing or constituting evidence

[397] Possession – the state of being dominated by evil spirits

[398] Concede – acknowledge, often reluctantly, as being true

[399] Clamorous – marked by sustained din

[400] Modulated – changed or varied the tone, pitch or intensity

[401] Concoct – devise using skill and intelligence

in there, maybe we can narrow it down."

"That doesn't give us much time to find what we're looking for, and we don't even really know what it is." Nick chewed on his lower lip. "It could be that red book, but what if something else is hidden in there?"

"We'll just have to take that chance. I hope we're smart enough to know what we're looking for when we see it."

"All right. I'm in." Nick scooped up another handful of popcorn. "But what about Dina? Shouldn't we keep her in the loop?"

"I don't know." Savannah plucked absentmindedly[402] at a loose thread hanging from her sleeve. "She's got a lot going on with Homecoming and everything. Plus, she told me that Jenna, Jake, and Carter showed up for her first planning meeting. What if we put her in some kind of danger by keeping her in the know? Maybe the three of them can sense things that we can't. Who knows?"

"I guess you're right," Nick acquiesced[403]. "If we do stumble across something, we can corner her at lunch and give her the details."

"Exactly." Savannah was glad they came to an accord[404]. "No need to worry her before we know anything."

"Okay, I'll meet you outside the library at 7:30." Nick locked eyes with her.

Nick's azure[405] gaze made butterflies flutter in her stomach. "You got it." Savannah wished she could set aside her growing feelings for her friend. This situation made any thoughts of romance seem petty by comparison.

Nick's mom, a petite blonde, peeked into the room. "Is everything okay in here, you two?"

"Everything's great, Mrs. Bishop." Savannah's face heated.

Nick's mother eyed them curiously, but she had a satisfied smile on her face. Mrs. Bishop appeared to be reveling[406] in the fact

---

[402] Absentmindedly – in a preoccupied manner

[403] Acquiesced – consented passively or without protest

[404] Accord – an agreement

[405] Azure – the color blue

[406] Reveling – taking great pleasure in

that Savannah was visiting. "You know you can come over any time you like, Savannah. It's always nice to have a pretty face stop by for a visit, isn't it, Nick?" She turned on her heel and took off down the hallway before her son could open his mouth.

Nick's ears were afire[407]. "Aren't moms awful?" Savannah tried to smooth over the awkward moment. The unexpected comment broke the usual friendly rapport[408] between them.

"Yeah." Nick ran his hand over his spiky hair. Silence passed between them. "So I was wondering if you wanted to go to the Homecoming Dance with me?" he spilled out all in a rush.

The butterflies flapped with a vengeance. The dance? With Nick? "But I thought someone else…" She thought back to their conversation in the library, and then it became clear. "Oh."

"But if you don't want to, it's okay. I really didn't want to go so much myself. I thought that it would be cool to go there because Dina…and because you…well…"

Did he think she was going to repudiate[409] the idea?

"Yes." Savannah stopped him from making more of a fool of himself. "I'd *love* to go with you."

Nick smiled shyly. "Okay. Good."

When had this happened? When had Nick had any affinity[410] for her besides friendship? He was smart and he was cute, in his own adorable spiky-blond-hair way. They were good study partners. She'd never thought in a million years, though, he would be enamored[411] of her—insipid[412], dependable Savannah who was logical to a fault. She had a proclivity[413] for high test scores and grade point averages rather than for dating and boys. At least, that's what she thought people believed about her.

The invitation to Homecoming hung between them and created an instant awkwardness. One minute they were good friends talking about research and planning their next move. The

---

[407] Afire – on fire, literally or figuratively

[408] Rapport – sympathetic compatibility

[409] Repudiate – refuse to have anything to do with

[410] Affinity – natural attraction, liking, or feeling of kinship

[411] Enamored – inspired with love, captivated

[412] Insipid - dull

[413] Proclivity – a natural propensity or inclination

next minute, they were both silently marveling[414] what this date actually meant.

"I'd better go" Savannah broke the silence first.

"Uh, okay, yeah." Nick avoided her gaze.

On impulse[415] Savannah leaned across the couch and gave Nick a quick kiss on the cheek. "I'll see you tomorrow?"

Nick caught her gaze and with new-found confidence answered, "Yes. Tomorrow."

She squeezed his hand and gave him a winsome[416] smile. They could date and still be friends, right? A wretched[417] thought climbed into her head. How was she going to break the news to Dina?

*

The darkness acted as her ally. Jenna climbed lithely[418] through her bedroom window, and the change began. Out on the barren rooftop, her hands elongated and transmuted[419] into claws, her nose extended forward and became a wolfish snout.

Jenna appreciated her new gifts—her heightened sense of smell and sight and her nimble[420] reflexes. Tonight she could indulge[421] her hunger. Tonight she would be sated.

Her stomach growled in anticipation. She bolted from the roof. Her werewolf body leapt easily from shingles to lawn with newly-formed limbs. She landed on the damp grass with a quiet expelling of air. Her claws dug into the soft earth beneath the lawn. She knew exactly where she was headed and took off at a blistering pace.

Jake warned her to be cautious. They craved human blood the most, but killing a human was risky. She needed to choose her victim carefully. This afternoon in gym she'd planned to take a

---

[414] Marveling – becoming filled with wonder or astonishment

[415] Impulse – a sudden desire

[416] Winsome – charming

[417] Wretched – characterized by woe or misery

[418] Lithely – marked by effortless grace

[419] Transmuted – changed from one form or state into another

[420] Nimble – quick, light, or agile in movement or action

[421] Indulge – yield to the desires and whims of

stray dog or maybe a couple of cats. They were plenteous[422] enough and made a satisfying meal. Her bloodlust for human flesh, however, was strong.

As she loped across the well-trimmed lawns of her neighborhood, she attracted minute[423] attention from her neighbors' dogs. A few stray barks from behind closed doors didn't bother her. Once she reached the end of the block, she darted into the strip of woods that separated her street from a public park.

She raced through the thin covering of trees and burst onto the playground, skittering dirt and sand everywhere. She let out a long howl, which echoed balefully[424] among the empty playground structures and reverberated all around her.

If she were lucky, she might just find…

There!

A pile of loose newspapers covered a homeless man sleeping on a park bench. The crumpled papers flapped in the breeze.

Jenna sneaked up behind the bench. She panted and waited. Hunting was new to her. She had instincts but hadn't perfected the skills. If she pounced on the man lying there on the park bench, he might scream. Dozens of homes lay just beyond the tree line. Someone might hear the noise and investigate. If she wanted this human, she needed to lure him into the woods. There, she could kill and devour him at her leisure[425] and hide his remains.

A long strand of drool escaped her mouth. Her hunger caused so much anguish[426], she might act without thinking. She connived[427] for a moment.

She trotted back to the woods and hid in a bush near the edge of the playground, about fifty yards from the bench. Jenna hoped she had enough human in her to make her plan work.

She whined[428] piteously[429] like a small child, rustled in the

---

[422] Plenteous - abundant

[423] Minute – exceptionally small, tiny

[424] Balefully – portending evil, ominously

[425] Leisure – at one's convenience

[426] Anguish – agonizing physical or mental pain

[427] Connived – schemed, plotted

[428] Whined – uttered a plaintive, high-pitched sound

[429] Piteously – in a way that arouses pity or compassion

bushes, and waited. Her sensitive ears picked up a slight crinkling of paper and stumbling footsteps. Her prey stumbled away from her with a half-empty gin bottle in his hand.

Jenna growled in frustration. Did it really matter if she attacked him out in the open or here in the woods? She rationalized[430] her change of plans. Her blood boiled for fresh human flesh, which was right there in front of her. No one could see them.

She exploded out of the arboreal[431] shrubs. Each footfall brought her closer and closer to her pusillanimous[432] prey. Her eyes focused like a laser on the man. He tipped back his head to take a drink from his bottle.

Jenna tackled him. The gin bottle fell to the concrete with a smash. The man's head hit the hard surface with a forcible[433] smack. Blood spattered on the ground. A rush of adrenaline filled her at the sight of the warm, red fluid. The man's body lay sprawled out in front of her and twitched spasmodically[434].

Jenna crept forward and snapped open her powerful jaws to make the kill.

---

[430] Rationalized – devised self-satisfying but incorrect reasons

[431] Arboreal – resembling a tree

[432] Pusillanimous – lacking courage, cowardly

[433] Forcible – powerful

[434] Spasmodically – fitfully, convulsively

CHAPTER NINE

Savannah yawned. At 7:15 in the morning she huddled outside the school and waited for the janitor to unlock the entrance. This early in the morning only the office doors were open. She didn't want to arouse suspicion by walking right past the school receptionist and Principal Morgan's office.

Getting up an hour earlier than her quotidian[435] routine had been difficult. Savannah liked her sleep. Anything less than seven hours left her enfeebled[436] during the school day.

"Hey, you." Nick bumped her with his shoulder. His hands were tucked in the pockets of his jeans. He gave her a shy smile.

"Hey," Savannah replied sanguinely[437] and bumped back against him. "Where'd you come from? I didn't see you pull up." In the adjacent[438] student parking lot her little silver Corolla sat all alone.

"My mom dropped me off on the way to her shift at the hospital. Gas prices being what they are these days, I wish I could hitch a ride with her more often."

Savannah nodded her head and validated[439] his statement. "Yeah, sucks, doesn't it?"

"Why haven't we ever set up some kind of car pool—you,

---

[435] Quotidian – recurring daily

[436] Enfeebled – deprived of strength

[437] Sanguinely - cheerfully

[438] Adjacent – next to, adjoining

[439] Validated – established the soundness of, corroborate

me, and Dina?"

"I'm not exactly on your way to school." Savannah pointed out the discrepancy[440] in his suggestion. They attended the same high school, but her house was in the opposite direction of Nick's. "You and Dina should talk about it, though. I'll bet she'd go for it."

"We could pick you up halfway," Nick offered. His argument wasn't cogent[441], and he knew it.

The janitor shuffled to the door and unlocked it from the inside. "Let's go," Savannah pulled open the glass door and entered the quiet corridor.

"Looks like Ms. Woodlawn's here." Nick followed closely behind.

The librarian, as was her habitual[442] practice, had propped open the door with a cinder block.

"I hope she lets us into that storage room or we are hosed." Savannah's words evinced[443] her desire to continue their research.

Their footsteps echoed in the empty hallway. Savannah nerves were on edge. What if Principal Morgan saw them? He could run into them at any moment.

"Why, good morning." Ms. Woodlawn surprised them both at the library entrance. Her reading glasses hung on a thin, black cord around her neck, which marred her elegant appearance: every hair in place, lipstick neatly applied, tweed skirt and silk blouse impeccable.

Savannah led the charge. "We were wondering if we could do some research in the storage room. Remember those books you showed us last week? A resource I found could really help us with our project."

"Is that so? Well, I'm glad to hear you're finding our little high school library sufficient[444] for your needs." She pulled the small key out of her skirt pocket. "It just so happens Principal Morgan wanted me to clear out that room today. Isn't that

---

[440] Discrepancy – disagreement between facts or claims

[441] Cogent – appealing to the intellect or powers of reasoning

[442] Habitual – chronic or usual

[443] Evinced – showed or demonstrated clearly

[444] Sufficient – being as much as is needed

auspicious[445]?"

"Clear it out?" Savannah gave Nick a meaningful look. They'd showed up at the library in the nick of time.

"Yes," Ms. Woodlawn answered curtly[446], an angry flicker in her eye. "Apparently, some parents found out what kinds of texts were in there and wanted them removed."

"Why?" Nick's question fell right in line with Savannah's thinking.

"Something about exposing young minds to disturbing materials or some such nonsense." Ms. Woodlawn shook her head in execration[447] at the ignorance. "If there was a book in particular you were interested in, perhaps I could help you."

"Well, we weren't quite sure..." Nick waffled.

Savannah interjected[448] with an effusion[449] of words. "No, that's all right Ms. Woodlawn. I'm sure we can find what we're looking for. We've only got thirty minutes." She glanced at the clock over the check-out desk, cognizant[450] of the late hour. "We'd really better get moving."

"All right." Ms. Woodlawn led them to the storage room door and unlocked the door. "Here you are."

The door swung in toward the dark recesses within. Ms. Woodlawn reached in to snap on the light.

"If you need anything, I'll be cataloguing some books over there." The librarian pointed to the fiction section near the entrance.

"Thanks." Savannah slipped into the room. She was eager to find what Principal Morgan didn't want her, and the rest of the Northeast High student body, to see.

Nick rushed in behind her and shut the door so only a small slit of light showed. "It doesn't sound like Ms. Woodlawn has any clue as to what Principal Morgan is up to."

"I know. But that's good news for us. We still have a chance

---

[445] Auspicious – attended by favorable circumstances

[446] Curtly – rudely brief or abrupt

[447] Execration – hate coupled with disgust

[448] Interjected – inserted between other elements

[449] Effusion – flood or outpouring

[450] Cognizant – fully informed, conscious

to get that book." She turned to the dusty stacks of antiquated[451] books she assiduously[452] searched through the other day. "I left it right here." The big crimson book, though, wasn't on top of the stack where she'd left it during her abridged[453] visit last week. In fact, she didn't see its distinctive binding anywhere in the piles of books in front of her.

"Which one is it?" Nick stood close behind her.

"I don't see it." All the books confounded[454] Savannah. "It's got to be here somewhere. It's a big red book with gold all over it. We've got to find it. I know it holds the key to everything." Savannah dove into the piles and hoped the book turned up.

"Are you sure it's not there?" Nick searched the rest of the storage room for any glimmer[455] of red.

"I don't know. It's gotta be here, Nick." Savannah clawed her way to the bottom of one pile and started on another. The storage room had been organized in piles and stacks when they entered, now it was a variegated[456] wreck of books, papers, and file folders.

"Ms. Woodlawn's gonna kill us if she sees what we've done to this place." Nick surveyed the little room they had razed[457].

"Not if they're going to be clearing it out this afternoon." Savannah glanced at her watch. "Only ten more minutes. Did you find it yet?"

"Nope." Nick flipped through a box of file folders stuffed with papers. "Hey, wait a minute. This is weird." He pulled a notebook out of the box and handled it as if it were an ancient artifact[458].

"What is it?" Savannah dropped the heavy book in her hands. She could sense something was afoot[459].

---

[451] Antiquated – very old, aged

[452] Assiduously – with care and persistence

[453] Abridged – short or limited in duration

[454] Confounded – confused, befuddled

[455] Glimmer – a faint manifestation or indication

[456] Variegated – having a variety of colors

[457] Razed – leveled to the ground, demolished

[458] Artifact – a remaining piece from an extinct culture or place

[459] Afoot – currently in progress

"Looks like somebody's notes. What would *this* be doing in *here?*" He gestured at the box clearly marked 'Library Records 1995-2005.'

"Let me see that." Savannah stood close to Nick as he leafed through the pages. She noted how tall he was and how virile[460] his body was next to hers. She felt safe and protected with him near. After yesterday's encounter with the principal, she was glad to have him with her this morning.

"Savannah, my gosh." His face paled. "They're werewolves."

"What?" Savannah suspected the three teenagers had been altered, but she'd never suspected something this ghastly[461]. She scanned Nick's face for confirmation his statement wasn't a fabrication[462]. "What does it say? Read it to me." She pulled at the edge of the notebook to get a look.

"There's a list of symptoms." He scanned the first couple of pages. "And there's sketch of some kind of circle with a star in the middle." He showed her the rough drawing in blue pen.

"A pentagram!" Savannah's insides turned to mush. She stared at the page. Jenna, Jake and Carter were all werewolves? *Could it be possible?*

Savannah stepped back. A laugh escaped her lips. "It's a joke."

"What?" Nick's face wore a mask of confusion.

"Yes, that has to be it," Savannah whispered to herself. Her logical[463] mind refused to accept the truth.

Worry reflected in his gaze. "It's not a joke, Savannah. Look." He forced the notebook into her hands. "Everything we've been talking about is right here."

Savannah touched the edges of the spiral-bound book. "It can't be. It's ludicrous[464]."

"It's true," Nick insisted. When she wouldn't take the notebook from him, he read it aloud. "The subject will experience personality changes and physical anomalies such as luminous eyes,

---

[460] Virile – characterized by energy and vigor

[461] Ghastly – inspiring shock or horror, terrifying

[462] Fabrication – a deliberately false or improbable account

[463] Logical – capable of or characterized by clear reasoning

[464] Ludicrous – completely devoid of wisdom or good sense

elongated incisors, and augmented[465] auditory[466] abilities. Other changes that may be noticeable: decreased ability to control anger, insatiable appetite, especially for raw meats, a desire to recruit others…"

Those words were the very description of Jenna. Savannah slowly came out of her state of shock. To negate[467] the facts would be foolish now. "You're right, Nick. You're right."

The jangle of the first bell made Savannah jump. Nick gently compressed[468] her arm with his hand to reassure[469] her.

"Put this in your backpack, Nick." Savannah could feel her pertinacity[470] returning. Even though the truth was hard to believe, she wasn't going to give up. If they had a werewolf problem at their high school, they had to deal with it. Those three people were a threat to the whole high school. They had to be stopped. "Principal Morgan already suspects that I know more than I should. That notebook wouldn't be safe with me."

He shoved the notebook into his backpack. "He *must* be involved in this. Right?" Nick asked rhetorically.

"I'm afraid so, Nick." Savannah validated[471] his thoughts.

A loud knock on the door startled them both. "Did you hear the first bell?" Ms. Woodlawn asked.

"Yes, we were just wrapping up in here." Savannah gathered her things.

The door swung open, and Nick managed to zip his backpack closed before Ms. Woodlawn entered.

"Well, let me lock up then." The librarian didn't seem to notice their nervousness. She waited patiently as Savannah and Nick filed out of the storage room. She turned off the light and locked the door.

"Thanks again for letting us look at those books one last

---

[465] Augmented – made greater in size, extent, or quantity

[466] Auditory – of or relating to hearing

[467] Negate – rule out, deny

[468] Compressed – pressed together or into a smaller space

[469] Reassure – restore confidence to

[470] Pertinacity – persistent determination

[471] Validated – found or tested the truth of something

time." Savannah gave the prim[472] Ms. Woodlawn a smile. "The final bell will ring in a couple of minutes." Ms. Woodlawn shooed them out of the library. "You two had better scoot."

Nick and Savannah split in different directions for class. Nick had P.E. in the gym, and Savannah had to ascend[473] the stairs for her computer lab.

"Let's meet tonight to look over that notebook." Savannah stopped on the first stair.

"This time, can we meet at your house?" Nick asked with a scintilla[474] of hope in his voice.

Remembering Mrs. Bishop's humiliating[475] remarks at Nick's house, Savannah agreed. She hoped her own mother knew better than to discuss her and Nick's relationship. Right now, Nick was her date to the Homecoming Dance. They hadn't discussed exactly what that meant. Were they dating? Or were they just friends?

Savannah was okay with the idea of remaining friends with the potential[476] for something more. Besides, with werewolves prowling around campus, they needed to be at the top of their game if they wanted to figure out a way to save the school. A real relationship might cloud their judgment.

"Stay away from Principal Morgan, Savannah," Nick warned as they parted ways in the congested[477] corridor. "Promise me you won't see him again without me." He might only be a seventeen-year-old high school kid, but Nick's protective[478] instincts must've kicked into high gear.

"I promise." Savannah was surprised at the vehemence[479] in Nick's voice. He seemed honestly frightened for her. Maybe their relationship was more serious than one date for Homecoming.

*

---

[472] Prim – strait-laced, prudish
[473] Ascend – go or move upward
[474] Scintilla – a minute amount or trace
[475] Humiliating – demeaning, puts to shame
[476] Potential – capable of being but not yet in existence
[477] Congested – overfilled or crowded
[478] Protective – showing a care
[479] Vehemence – intensity or forcefulness of expression

Principal Morgan stared at a large red book sitting in the middle of his desk. He managed to wrest[480] it out of the storage room before those kids had a chance to look at it again. That was a close call. How had they happened upon the book he hid there? And what had they witnessed to interest them in such research in the first place?

He rose from his swivel chair and removed a cheap, framed print of the New York skyline that adorned[481] the wall behind his desk. A safe door made of brushed metal was hidden beneath. He turned the knob to dial in the numerical[482] combination. The door popped open with a muffled click. He grabbed the weighty tome off of his desk and heaved it inside. Then, he unlocked the lowest drawer in his desk. When the drawer slid open, he frowned.

Where was it?

Didn't he put it back in his desk afterwards? He couldn't remember clearly. He thought he did, but now the drawer stood empty. He must have been remiss[483] and left it behind. His face became pallid[484] at the thought, and his bow tie suddenly suffocated him. He pulled at his collar and plopped down into his chair. It couldn't be. He couldn't have forgotten. He ran his fingers through his hair.

His phone rang. The nasal[485] voice of the receptionist was on the other end, "There's someone here to see you, Mr. Morgan. A Mr....?"

No more time to think about it. He'd have to retrace[486] his steps later.

"Yes, let him in."

Before his visitor could walk through the door, he closed the safe door and spun the dial. He exhaled[487] with a weary sigh. His hand rested on the dial. Would that be a good enough hiding place?

---

[480] Wrest – obtain by seizing forcefully

[481] Adorned – decorated, made beautiful

[482] Numerical – expressed in or counted by numbers

[483] Remiss – lax in a attending to duty, negligent

[484] Pallid – having an abnormally pale or wan complexion

[485] Nasal – a resonant sound produced through the nose

[486] Retrace – go back over again

[487] Exhaled – breathed out

For now, it would have to do. He replaced the picture to cover the safe opening and turned to greet his visitor. He hoped he'd made the right decision.

His guest entered the office. Principal Morgan reached out his hand in greeting. "Welcome, Daniel. I've been expecting you."

CHAPTER TEN

"Oh my gosh, Savannah, when were you going to tell me? Never?" Dina sat down next to her in the cafeteria at lunch. Her earrings bobbed fitfully[488].

Savannah face heated. "Nick asked me to the dance yesterday. What was I supposed to do, call you immediately afterwards?"

"Yes." Dina let out an exasperated sigh. "When your cute study-buddy asks you out on a date…"

"It's only a dance."

Dina glared at her. "As I was saying, when you get asked out on a date, it's big news. I mean super huge. That's something you call your best friend about, okay?"

"Okay." Savannah felt summarily[489] chastised[490].

"So, is he going to take you out to dinner first? What kind of dress are you going to buy? Did he try to kiss you?" Dina assailed[491] her with questions, not giving Savannah a chance to answer any of them.

"Did who try to kiss whom?" Nick demanded as he thunked his tray of cafeteria food down on the table.

Savannah's expression must have been the give away. Nick took a look at her from across the table and guessed. "Geez, Dina.

---

[488] Fitfully – irregularly, spasmodically

[489] Summarily – without delay

[490] Chastised – criticized severely, rebuked

[491] Assailed – Attacked verbally

We're going to the dance together, okay?" Nick gave Savannah a reassuring wink. "End of story."

"All right. I get it." Dina frowned. "I'll leave you two lovebirds alone."

"Dina!" Savannah's face heated.

"Here, would this be better?" Nick got up from his seat beside Dina, <u>adroitly</u>[492] pushed his tray across the table, and sat next to Savannah. He threw an arm over her shoulder and pulled her close.

Dina rolled her eyes, took a last sip of milk, and cleared her things from the table. "Like I said, I'll leave you two lovebirds alone." She smiled at her two friends <u>nestling</u>[493] in the cafeteria and left.

Savannah sat frozen on the bench, unable to react to his <u>impertinence</u>[494].

Nick put his arm around her in front of the whole school.

He squeezed her shoulders and dropped his arm. "Sorry about that, Savannah. Sometimes Dina really knows how to <u>incite</u>[495] my <u>wrath</u>[496]."

She shrugged off his show of affection. Clearly, he had done that for Dina's sake. It didn't mean anything. Right?

She scooted away and shook off the feel of his arm around her. She wasn't completely <u>immune</u>[497] to the affects of his closeness, however. "I know what you mean. She can push my buttons sometimes, too."

"I want to clear something up with you." Nick's <u>limpid</u>[498] gaze burned bright blue.

Savannah braced herself for the 'we're just friends' speech. The invite to the Homecoming Dance had been nothing more than a friendly gesture. Savannah knew it.

"This dance? It's a date," he said in his matter-of-fact science

---

[492] Adroitly – dexterously, deftly

[493] Nestling – pressing close as in affection, snuggling

[494] Impertinence – inappropriate playfulness

[495] Incite – provoke, urge on

[496] Wrath - anger

[497] Immune – not affected by a given influence

[498] Limpid – calm, untroubled

voice. "I'm asking you out. I'm picking you up in my car, I'm taking you out to dinner, and we're going to the dance. Got it?"

Savannah swallowed. His statement germinated[499] a bad case of butterflies in her stomach. He really liked her! "Okay." She couldn't think of anything else to say.

"When I come over this afternoon, we can talk about it more." Nick dug into his lunch. "Don't worry, I'll remember to bring the notebook."

Her moment of giddiness[500] disappeared at the mention of the notebook. What else would they find inside? Whose choppy script[501] filled those pages? Who had stashed in the storage room? And what happened to that red book? Savannah was certain that book held some very important information about what was going on at their school.

*

Dina tossed her lunch into the heavy-duty garbage can near the cafeteria entrance and stacked her tray. Her thoughts drifted to the Homecoming Dance and the surprising news her two best friends would be going together.

Where did that leave her? Planning the dance made it incumbent[502] that she be present at the event. She'd never even thought about looking for a date. She'd assumed Nick and Savannah would be there, so they could all hang out like they usually did. Nick and Savannah going together left her as the third wheel. She had a morose[503] dilemma[504].

She was happy for them, but also covetous[505]. What she wouldn't give to have some guy show interest in her beyond asking for the answers to last night's math problems.

"Hey, Dina, how's it going?"

The appearance of Carter startled her. He might have

---

[499] Germinated – caused to grow or sprout
[500] Giddiness – silliness, lightheartedness
[501] Script – handwriting
[502] Incumbent – obligatory
[503] Morose – gloomy
[504] Dilemma – a problem that seems to defy a satisfactory solution
[505] Covetous – marked by extreme desire to acquire or possess

seemed normal at the meeting, but she grew wary. A vestige[506] of doubt remained about him.

"What's up, Carter?" Dina hated to admit it, but Carter was pretty cute for a junior. He was tall and had the lanky physique of a quarterback. The thought that he was the perfect date for Homecoming flashed through her mind. She dismissed it, though, as a lunatic's[507] dream.

"I wanted to ask you something."

"Ask away." Dina tugged on one of her earrings. Nerves got the best of her so easily.

"I was wondering if committee members were allowed to bring dates to the dance."

"Uh, of course. Most of our work happens before the dance even starts. That wouldn't be a problem." How daunting[508] to have Carter focus on her so completely. She fought hard to keep her equanimity[509].

"Good."

"Do have anyone in mind?" Dina couldn't believe those words came out of her mouth.

"I might." His gaze intensified. Not scary or glowing or anything. Just intense.

His solicitous[510] attentions made Dina's heart flutter.

"Hey, Carter!" Jake shouted from the jock table. "You got a minute?"

Carter looked in Jake's direction.

Dina let out a sigh. Yes, she wouldn't mind going with a junior at all. She had to admit, she was secretly pleased their research had gotten them nowhere. Maybe nothing had been wrong with Jenna, Carter, and Jake, and they had overreacted to the speculations[511] swirling around school.

"I'll be right there." Carter turned back in Dina's direction. "I'll catch up with you later, okay?"

---

[506] Vestige – an indication that something has been present

[507] Lunatic – an insane or crazy person

[508] Daunting – discouraging through fear

[509] Equanimity – the quality of being calm, even-tempered

[510] Solicitous – showing hovering attentiveness

[511] Speculations – reasoning based on inconclusive evidence

"Okay." Dina's heart raced. A date with a varsity football player would be quite a coup[512].

Carter smiled a beatific[513] smile that made Dina melt. Her knees wobbled, and she grabbed the edge of the counter for support.

As he trotted toward the jock table, he gave Dina a wave and a wink.

Dina walked out of the cafeteria and hoped no one could sense the maelstrom[514] of emotions that coursed through her. Best not to say anything to Savannah. She wouldn't understand her attraction to a jock, especially one they suspected of being changed in some way. Besides, there wasn't anything going on between her and Carter. *Yet.*

Dina felt a connection with Carter that stretched beyond friendly conversation. If Carter stayed active on the Homecoming Committee, maybe she would have a chance to find out the depth[515] of that connection.

---

[512] Coup – a brilliantly executed stratagem, a triumph

[513] Beatific – resembling or befitting an angel or saint

[514] Maelstrom – whirlpool of extraordinary size or violence

[515] Depth – the degree of richness or intensity

CHAPTER ELEVEN

Activity bustled[516] during Homecoming Week at Northeast High. Cheerleaders decorated the football players' lockers with green and yellow streamers and posters of the Northeast Bulls trampling the rival South Hill Knights. They delivered baskets of cookies and cupcakes, balloon bouquets, and even pizzas in the middle of class to each player.

Savannah never understood why jocks received such special treatment. Why didn't students on the honor roll get rewarded with free food instead of a mention in the quarterly newsletter? Acrimony[517] crept into her heart over the partisanship[518].

The Homecoming Dance on Friday would at least be some consolation[519]. She'd picked out a gorgeous dress, and Nick had hinted at a very special evening for their first official date. Since he'd asked her to the dance over two weeks ago, their relationship had changed subtly[520]. Dina had been so busy with the Homecoming committee that Nick and Savannah spent a lot of time alone—doing homework, talking, researching.

However, their werewolf research had come to a halt. The notebook provided very little useful or enlightening[521] information,

---

[516] Bustle – excited and often noisy activity, a stir

[517] Acrimony – bitter, sharp animosity

[518] Partisanship – biased in support of a party, group, or cause

[519] Consolation – the state of being comforted

[520] Subtly – so slight as to be difficult to detect or describe

[521] Enlightening – informative, instructive

precluding[522] them from learning much more. The notebook only corroborated[523] that someone else knew what was going on at Northeast High and that they were definitely dealing with werewolves.

Sketches of claws, teeth, and other werewolf parts took up a dozen or so pages in the notebook. Notes described werewolf abilities and detailed a few historical references—the supposed origin[524] of the werewolf and its modern-day equivalent[525]. They could find no explanation as to how one became a werewolf, no notes on specific students suspected of being werewolves, and no details on how to change a werewolf back into a human.

Luckily, no more students had disappeared in the last couple of weeks. Savannah and Nick had watched Jenna, Jake, and Carter closely, looking for signs of a werewolf to manifest. They also kept tabs on Dina.

Dina had been happier this week than Savannah had ever seen her. Giddy almost. When Savannah questioned her, Dina revealed nothing and would only say that she was having a really good week. Savannah decided it must be the excitement of all her Homecoming plans coming to fruition. Dina's hard work was about to pay off.

A skinny blonde cheerleader bedecked[526] in her green and gold uniform waltzed into Savannah's physics classroom encumbered[527] with a pizza box and a two-liter soda bottle. The pretty girl pranced over to Scott Holmsby, a defensive tackle.

"Gotta keep your strength up, Scotty." The girl pouted.

A few of Savannah's fellow students grumbled as the tempting odor of tomato sauce and cheese wafted through the room.

Mr. Dunleavy stood next to the white board and frowned. "Ms. Smith, I don't mind you interrupting our class for a special delivery, but the talking isn't necessary." Their teacher had shown

---

[522] Precluding – preventing, keeping from happening
[523] Corroborated – strengthened or supported with other evidence
[524] Origin – the place where something begins
[525] Equivalent – being essential equal
[526] Bedecked – decorated, adorned
[527] Encumbered – impeded by a heavy load

little tolerance[528] for the food deliveries that plagued his classes for the past couple of days.

"All right, I'm going." The cheerleader sneered.

Heaven forbid the brat couldn't coddle[529] her assigned player for the rest of the period.

"Thanks." Scotty lifted the lid of the cardboard box.

Savannah's stomach growled. Thirty minutes remained until lunch, and the delicious odor of pizza was intoxicating. The craziness may only last for one week, but Savannah thought it was pretty insufferable[530] nonetheless.

Scotty reached a meaty paw into the box and seemed intent on retrieving a slice.

"Mr. Holmsby!" Mr. Dunleavy said curtly. "We do not eat in this class."

"But…"

"You know the rules. Please place the box under your desk until the lunch break."

"It'll probably be cold by then."

"And I should care because…?"

Savannah snickered in derision[531]. She was full of felicity[532] to see one of the jocks get his comeuppance. Even for something silly like denying Scott Holmsby a chance to eat a hot pizza. She wondered how Dina could stand to work with the jocks and their cheerleader counterparts. They believed they deserved special treatment. It made her sick.

Most of the Homecoming Committee consisted of cheerleaders and their athletic boyfriends. Although Savannah looked forward to the dance, she was ambivalent[533] about the students who put it together. She viewed Dina as a paragon[534] of tolerance for shouldering that kind of responsibility. Thing was,

---

[528] Tolerance – capacity to endure something, especially pain or hardship

[529] Coddle – treat indulgently

[530] Insufferable – difficult or impossible to endure, intolerable

[531] Derision – contemptuous or jeering laughter, ridicule

[532] Felicity – great happiness, bliss

[533] Ambivalent – characterized by a mixture of feelings

[534] Paragon – a model of excellence or perfection of a kind

Dina didn't seem to mind interacting with the popular crowd one bit.

Savannah mulled that over. Dina had changed in the few weeks she'd headed the committee. At lunch Dina preferred[535] to have pow-wows with the popular crowd. Nick didn't seem to be bothered by it as much as Savannah. Dina always had an interest in finding a way into the popular clique. Savannah supposed it was no surprise to Nick when she finally succeeded to some degree.

For Savannah, the transition[536] had been difficult. She and Dina had been friends for years—supporting each other, studying together, competing for the best grades in class. She had trouble letting her go and giving her old friend some space.

Savannah couldn't help but worry when Dina spent more and more time with Carter Rittenhouse, suspected werewolf. She and Nick had kept that revelation[537] under wraps until they could excavate[538] more information from the notebook. Now, however, Savannah couldn't stay silent any longer and felt compelled to warn her friend. She hoped it wouldn't turn into a polemical[539] conversation.

Savannah broached[540] the topic. "Dina, did I see you with Carter yesterday? Sitting in his car after school?"

"Yeah. What's wrong with that?" Dina fulminated[541] at the accusation[542] buried in Savannah's questions. "Am I not allowed to make any friends beside you and Nick?"

Savannah let the sharp comment roll off her back, not wanting to push Dina further away. "I'm worried, Dina. Remember a few weeks ago? How odd he was acting?"

Dina cut her off. "And there was nothing to it. He's completely normal, and so are his friends."

Before Savannah could defend her position, Dina grabbed

---

[535] Preferred – liked better or valued more highly

[536] Transition – passage from one form, state, or style to another

[537] Revelation – an enlightening or astonishing disclosure

[538] Excavate – expose or uncover as if by digging

[539] Polemical – of or relating to a controversy or argument

[540] Broached – brought up a subject for discussion or debate

[541] Fulminated – issued a thunderous verbal attack or denunciation

[542] Accusation – assertion that someone is guilty of an offense

her tray off the table and joined a very full table of popular students.

Nick appeared, his tray loaded with the usual half dozen rolls and peanut butter packets. "What's her problem?" He sat across from Savannah.

"I ticked her off." She picked <u>perfunctorily</u>[543] at her cheese sandwich. "I was just asking about her and Carter..."

"Savannah, I thought we agreed to leave her out of this until we knew more." Nick slathered a roll with peanut butter.

"I know, but I'm worried about her."

"She'll be okay. We've been keeping an eye on her." He took a gulp of milk. "If anything funky was going on, I think we'd know about it."

"I'm not so sure. And now I've made her mad at me." She took <u>deliberate</u>[544] bites of her sandwich.

"She'll get over it. You guys have been friends forever. She'll be here any minute and then you'll see...You think she's going to dump you to hang out with her new cheerleader friends?"

Savannah shook her head, but deep down she <u>abjured</u>[545] Nick's thoughts on the matter. She was anxious that her smart, fun friend would fall in with the popular crowd permanently. They both had goals and dreams that went way beyond high school. A relationship with Carter and his friends could have a <u>pernicious</u>[546] influence on the rest of Dina's life.

Someone dropped a tray and Savannah jolted. She'd been lost in her thoughts for a few minutes. It was <u>disquieting</u>[547]. She had physics class next and hoped she didn't drift off in her college <u>preparatory</u>[548] course. She and Nick needed to ferret out more information about werewolves. Now. Her grades this semester needed to stay up to snuff if she intended to seriously compete for valedictorian. She rubbed her fingers at her temples. If she didn't find out something soon, she feared her head would explode.

---

[543] Perfunctorily – acting with indifference

[544] Deliberate – unhurried in action and often slowly

[545] Abjured – formally rejected or disavowed

[546] Pernicious – causing great harm, destructive

[547] Disquieting – troubling, causing mental discomfort

[548] Preparatory – introductory, preliminary

*

Dina sat next to Carter in the cafeteria. Since her argument with Savannah the other day, she didn't see the need to split her friendship between the two groups. Besides, Carter asked her to be his date for the dance, and she wanted to spend any available free time with him.

She picked at her food and listened rapturously[549] to her date.

"So there's going to be this really cool party on Thursday..."

"Thursday?"

He delineated[550] some of the guests. "Jenna's going. Jake's gonna be there, too."

"But school's the next day," Dina repined[551].

"Yeah? So what?" Carter dismissed her worries.

Dina didn't want to disappoint Carter. "I guess it's not a big deal. Anyway, we'll be so busy on Friday. You've got the game, and I have to supervise the set-up."

"Exactly. We'll be too beat to really have a good time."

"I suppose."

Jenna sidled up to their table carrying a tray with two large portions of meatloaf and a carton of milk. Kind of a strange lunch for a teenage girl. But Dina welcomed her as if she were her new best friend.

"So, what're you two talking about?" Jenna asked blithely[552], scooting from one end of the bench toward Dina. She stabbed a large chunk of meatloaf with her fork and lifted it to her mouth.

"The party on Thursday," Carter replied.

"You're coming, right?" Jenna cajoled[553] and bit down on her oversized bit of loaf.

Dina wavered.

"Oh, come on." Jenna was dogmatic[554] about the importance of the party. "It'll be such a blast!" She speared another huge piece

---

[549] Rapturously – filled with great joy, ecstatically

[550] Delineated - described

[551] Repined – complained, fretted

[552] Blithely – in a carefree or lighthearted manner

[553] Cajoled – urged with gentle and repeated appeals

[554] Dogmatic – characterized by arrogant assertion

of food. That girl had quite an appetite.

Dina looked from Carter to Jenna. She wanted to be part of their clique so badly she could taste it. A date with Carter to the dance was only a small step. Showing up at a cool party would probably cement her relationship. If Jenna were going, why couldn't she?

Carter prodded Dina. "So, you'll go with me on Thursday?"

"Sure, why not?" Dina acceded[555], cleaving[556] to her cute football player. Everything she'd ever wanted was starting to happen. She was part of the popular crowd, she had an adorable guy taking her to the dance, and now she'd been invited to an exclusive[557] party.

"Cool." Jenna opened her milk carton with a snap.

"I'll pick you up at ten," Carter said.

"Why so late?" Dina worried she wouldn't be able to slip out of her house so late on a school night. What kind of excuse would her parents believe?

Absolutely nothing.

"That's when the party starts." Jenna shrugged.

Dina let loose a malediction[558] in her head. Her parents knew how busy she'd been in the last few weeks, trying to keep up her grades and organizing the dance. They would never let her go out with some strange boy so late on a school night. Her parents' mores[559] were two decades behind.

Carter drank the contents of his milk carton in one gulp. "Look, do you want to go or not?"

Dina didn't want Carter to back out of their date. "What'll I tell my parents?"

"Tell 'em you have to work on decorating[560] the gym before the dance," Carter suggested.

---

[555] Acceded – gave consent, often at the insistence of another

[556] Cleaving – adhering, clinging

[557] Exclusive – excluding much or all of a particular group

[558] Malediction – curse

[559] Mores – moral attitudes

[560] Decorating – furnishing or adorning with something ornamental

Jenna agreed with the pretense[561]. "They want their little girl to organize the best dance ever, don't they?"

Dina knew her parents were proud of her academic accomplishments in school. Getting an important job like the Homecoming Coordinator only furthered[562] their belief that their daughter was on the right track to the Ivy League. Carter had posed a good excuse. One her parents would swallow hook, line, and sinker.

"Sounds like a plan." Dina smiled. Her fears about being caught were assuaged[563].

A wicked gleam shone in Carter's eye. "That's my girl." He put his arm around her.

Dina sighed and leaned against his muscular frame. Now *this* was what high school was all about. This exculpation[564] would totally work. When had her parents had any reason to be suspicious of her?

---

[561] Pretense – a professed but feigned reason

[562] Furthered – helped the progress of, advanced

[563] Assuaged – relieved, pacified, calmed

[564] Exculpation – excuse or defense

CHAPTER TWELVE

"Hey, look, there's Dina." Nick indicated[565] the football table.

Dina sat next to Jenna and Carter, and Carter's arm was around her.

"What are we going to do?" Savannah lost the rest of her appetite at the sight of her friend cuddling close to a possible werewolf.

"Are you thinking what I'm thinking?" Nick bit into a perfectly globular[566] red apple.

"We have to stick to her like glue." If they didn't help Dina now, she'd end up embroiled[567] in the werewolf mess.

"Exactly."

"What if he's just getting close to her so he can kidnap her, like Jenna?"

"Where would he take her? We still don't know much more than when we first started this whole thing."

"My intuition[568] tells me that the drawing of the pentagram was an important part of the puzzle."

"What does a pentagram tell us about where Jenna disappeared to for three days? How can we stop these creeps from

---

[565] Indicated – pointed out
[566] Globular – spherical, having the shape of a globe
[567] Embroiled – forced into some kind of situation or condition
[568] Intuition – instinctive knowing

taking over our school?" Nick's voice rose an <u>octave</u>[569]. His words <u>pervaded</u>[570] half the cafeteria, and half a dozen students stared at them.

"I don't know." Savannah touched his arm to calm him. "But since Carter seems to have taken a liking to our friend, we should probably take turns keeping an eye on Dina. Don't you think?"

"You mean like surveillance?"

"Yeah."

"How are we going to do that? Stake out her house with a pot of coffee and a box of donuts?" Nick's <u>penchant</u>[571] for sarcasm intensified in a crisis.

"If that's what it takes." Nick's gaze narrowed when Dina leaned her head in <u>adoration</u>[572] on Carter's shoulder. "How can she act like that? She knows what we're researching. She knows something's wrong."

"I don't know if she believes it anymore. Or maybe werewolves have a way of luring in their victims. Like a trance or something."

Nick took another look at Dina and Carter. "Maybe." He didn't sound convinced.

"I'll watch her tonight. You take Wednesday, and I'll be on Thursday." With that kind of <u>persistence</u>[573] they might be able to <u>prevent</u>[574] a <u>catastrophe</u>[575].

"What about Friday?"

"We'll both be at the dance together, and Dina will have to be there. She's in charge, right?"

"Right."

Savannah created a <u>coherent</u>[576] plan for her evening. She'd follow Dina home from school and watch her house until about six

---

[569] Octave – musical interval of eight notes
[570] Pervaded – was present throughout, permeated
[571] Penchant – definite liking, strong inclination
[572] Adoration – profound love or regard
[573] Persistence – continuing determination
[574] Prevent – keep from happening
[575] Catastrophe – a complete failure, a fiasco
[576] Coherent – orderly, logical, consistent

o'clock or so. For a few hours, though, Savannah would have to be at home. Around nine-thirty or ten, she'd sneak out of the house and plant herself across the street from Dina's house. She'd pulled all-nighters before; this wouldn't be much different. She'd just load up on caffeinated soda and lots of sugar.

*

For two unsuccessful, sleepy nights Savannah and Nick kept a vigil[577] at Dina's house. Parked across the street under the darkness of an oak tree, each watched the house for any sign of intrusion[578]. Staying awake at school all day after manning a ten-hour stake out was no way to live. Savannah managed to stay alert chugging several energy drinks between classes; Nick relied on one candy bar per period. Neither method worked well.

Thursday night changed all that.

Savannah had armed herself with a thermos of coffee dosed with a liberal[579] amount of milk and sugar. She'd arrived at Dina's house a few minutes before ten, dressed warmly in jeans, a long-sleeved t-shirt, and a heavy sweater. The late October nights were bordering on glacial[580], and she couldn't keep the car engine running all night in order to have heat.

Preparing herself for another monotonous[581] night, she couldn't believe her eyes when Dina stepped onto the porch and gave her mother a quick hug. Where was she going this time of night?

Suspicions immediately aroused, Savannah pulled out her cell phone and called Nick. They'd pledged[582] to keep one another updated if anything strange happened.

Before she could finish dialing, a motorcycle pulled up to the curb. The figure on the bike climbed off and pulled off a jet-black helmet.

Carter Rittenhouse.

He strode up to the porch, shook Mrs. Moore's hand, and

---

[577] Vigil – period of observing, surveillance
[578] Intrusion – entrance by force or without permission
[579] Liberal – generous in amount
[580] Glacial – extremely cold, icy
[581] Monotonous – tediously repetitive
[582] Pledged – promised solemnly

they chatted for a few seconds.

What in the heck was going on? Why was Mrs. Moore letting Dina meet up with Carter this late on a school night? Although it appeared to be innocuous[583], Savannah couldn't squelch the feeling of dread that lodged like a lump in her throat.

Savannah finished dialing and kept a close eye on the two teenagers across the street. The phone rang four times. Nick's voicemail picked up.

Where was he?

They'd made an explicit[584] agreement to keep their cell phones on at all times. She left a quick message about what she'd witnessed and asked Nick to call her back as soon as possible.

Mrs. Moore closed the front door. Dina and Carter stepped off the porch holding hands. Carter handed her his helmet and helped her strap it on. Carter got back on the motorcycle, started it, and waited for Dina to climb on behind him.

Savannah waited anxiously for her cell phone to ring.

Where was Nick?

The motorcycle sped off. Savannah couldn't wait any longer to get a hold of Nick. She had to follow them before they disappeared. Carter headed to the outskirts[585] of town, around the big city park and toward the woods that edged Centerville on its southern boundaries.

Anxiety excruciated[586] Savannah's stomach.

Was this it? Was Carter going to kidnap Dina?

Although she despaired[587] for Dina, she was also sequacious[588]. What if Carter led her right to the heart of the werewolf pack? She couldn't miss out on that opportunity. She prayed Nick would call.

Worried Carter might notice her, Savannah eased her foot off the gas. The road he chose didn't have many exits, so she was confident she wouldn't lose them. On the straightaways Savannah

---

583 Innocuous – harmless

584 Explicit – fully and clearly expressed or defined

585 Outskirts – part or region remote from the central district

586 Excruciated – inflicted severe pain on, tortured

587 Despaired – abandoned or gave up hope

588 Sequacious – ready to be led, disposed to follow another

caught glimpses of the motorcycle's red taillights. He must've been speeding up because she receded[589] further from them with each passing minute. After a long section of s-curves, Savannah saw nothing but black in front of her.

She'd lost them.

Frantic[590], she sped up and hoped they were only a little bit ahead. After a couple of miles, she realized they'd turned off somewhere. She pulled onto the shoulder to turn around, and her phone rang. She slammed her car into park and answered the call.

Thank God it was Nick.

"Nick! I lost them!" Savannah thought her voice sounded strangely high-pitched and filled with apprehension[591].

"What? Lost who?"

"Where have you been? I can't find them!" Despondency[592] filled her. Their attempt to keep Dina safe was futile[593]. How could she be so naive to think she and Nick could beat out a pack of werewolves?

"Is Dina okay?"

"No! She got on this motorcycle with Carter, and now I'm out in the middle of nowhere." Her words spilled out in a panicked rush and jumbled all together. "I have no idea where they went. Nick, I have to find her!"

"Slow down. Tell me where you are."

Savannah worried that each minute she wasted on the phone with Nick put Dina further out of her reach. "I've got to go. I'll call you back later." She truncated[594] the call and revved up her engine. She popped her car into drive and skidded back onto the road. Gravel skittered under the tires as she wheeled the Corolla around. Dina couldn't be that far away.

Where exactly did she lose them? How much time had elapsed[595]?

---

[589] Receded – moved back or away from

[590] Frantic – excessively agitated

[591] Apprehension – fearful or uneasy anticipation of the future

[592] Despondency – depression of spirits from loss of hope, courage

[593] Futile – producing no result or effect

[594] Truncated – shortened by cutting off

[595] Elapsed – slipped by, passed

Her mind raced and her pulse throbbed. She pressed down on the gas as if she were a Formula One racecar driver. Her poor car squealed in protest to meet her demands, but the exigency[596] of Dina's situation required the extra speed.

Her phone rang. She ignored it. Driving fast and keeping a lookout for the missing motorcycle took all of her concentration. "Sorry, Nick."

She noticed a dirt road on the left. A faded wooden sign proclaimed[597] she was entering the Centerville Recreational Area. She took the turn at a good clip. The rear end fishtailed on the gravel, but Savannah brought the car under her control. The road disappeared into a forest of gray and black trees. Ahead in the sky, the full, lustrous[598] moon rose over the line of pines and oaks.

How far did this road go? Was she wasting her time searching? Did she give Carter an opportunity to get away by diverting[599] down this bleak[600] and badly-maintained road?

Her headlights bounced off something metallic. Not right on the road, but off to the left in the woods. She braked hard and her seatbelt tensed[601] across her chest.

Was that a motorcycle?

Savannah swept under the passenger seat. She'd tucked a flashlight there in case she'd needed it during her stake out. She wrapped her fingers around its cylindrical heaviness. In these primeval[602] woods far from town, it would be inconceivable[603] to find her way around without it.

She climbed out and switched on the flashlight. The beam of light played across the underbrush. She methodically scanned the flashlight back and forth where she thought she saw the reflection[604].

---

[596] Exigency – pressing or urgent situation

[597] Proclaimed – announced officially

[598] Lustrous – having a sheen or glow

[599] Diverting – turning aside from a course or direction

[600] Bleak – gloomy and somber

[601] Tensed – make or become taut, tight

[602] Primeval – in an earliest or original state

[603] Inconceivable – totally unlikely

[604] Reflection – light or sound being thrown back from a surface

Bingo!

The light bounced off a large metal object. Not a motorcycle, but a car partially hidden behind a clump of bushes. A very familiar car.

Savannah's stomach lurched uneasily. Only one car in the school lot looked like this one, and it belonged to Principal Morgan.

The shabby, ding-covered Volkswagen Bug had a conspicuous bright red paint job that was incongruous[605] to the hulking, bow-tie wearing principal. Principal Morgan *should* drive a conservative two-door sedan, but yet he drove to work everyday in this throwback to the Hippie era.

Her belief that Principal Morgan was involved in the whole werewolf affair was irrevocable[606]. The culmination[607] of their investigation ended here. Savannah had picked the right turn-off. Somewhere down this road she'd find the motorcycle, Carter, and Dina.

Without any further hesitation, she hopped back into her car and drove further down the road. Her phone rang again. This time she answered it.

"Hey." She worked to keep the panic out of her voice.

"Where are you?" Nick's voice exploded in her ear.

"We were right, Nick. I didn't want to believe it, but we were right." Her teeth jarred in her mouth as the tires struck a particularly deep pothole in the road.

"Tell me where you are. You're freaking me out." Nick sounded so far away. She was alone out here in the woods, but she couldn't let down Dina. This might be her only chance to save her friend.

The phone crackled in her ear, and she heard only snippets of Nick's demands.

"Nick!" She was losing her cell connection. "Are you there?"

Nothing but dead silence answered her. She tossed the phone aside and swore at the primitive[608] cell service. The road

---

[605] Incongruous – incompatible, inconsistent

[606] Irrevocable – impossible to retract

[607] Culmination – a concluding action

[608] Primitive – primary or basic

ended abruptly in a small parking lot. She slammed on her brakes. Her heart sank when she saw Carter's motorcycle parked in front of her.

She couldn't doubt her suspicions now. Dina was in danger.

*

"Where in hell are we going?" Carter dragged Dina through the woods. She wasn't willing to abide[609] his harsh treatment for much longer. First, he gave her a terrorizing ride on his motorcycle and now he forced her on a strenuous[610] hike into the woods.

"To the party." Carter's earlier benevolence[611] toward her disappeared. He grew more demanding and less tolerant of her questions.

"But we're so far in the woods. I didn't see any other cars back there." Dina wasn't insentient[612]. As much as she wanted to believe Carter was bringing her into the fold of the popular clique, she could see now something had been seriously wrong with her judgment. His grip was like iron. When she tried to pull free, he only clamped down harder.

Dina's mind cleared.

This is what happened to Jenna. This is where they took her.

Her sharp intake of breath split the quiet night air. She shied away from Carter, and he aggressively[613] sunk his fingers into the soft flesh of her forearm.

"You're hurting me." Her emotions had swung from pure joy to the utmost[614] fear in only a few minutes. How could she have been so blind?

Savannah and Nick had been right.

"Shut up, Dina. It's too late to do anything about it."

"Do anything about what?" Panic drowned her.

"Didn't your friends tell you? We weren't sure how much they told you about us." Carter yanked her into a clearing and pushed her into the dirt. "It doesn't matter now."

---

[609] Abide – put up with, tolerate

[610] Strenuous – requiring great energy or effort

[611] Benevolence – kindliness, lenience

[612] Insentient – devoid of feeling, consciousness, animation

[613] Aggressively – assertively, boldly, harshly

[614] Utmost – of the highest or greatest degree

Dina broke her fall with her hand. She heard a sickening snap of bone as her arm gave way. In agony, she clutched her injured wrist to her chest. Her mind became a swirl of fear, pain, and confusion. She couldn't think straight. She scrambled for footing in the loose soil. Dizzy, she stumbled toward the trees, her good arm stretched out in front of her.

Where did Carter go? She had to run away. Now.

A discord[615] of chanting and howling erupted all around her, stopping her dead in her tracks. Goosebumps rose on her skin at the feral sounds. She froze and closed her eyes as her hope of escaping was extinguished[616]. She was too aghast[617] to open them and see what might be waiting for her out there in the dark.

A sharp throb of pain exploded in her arm. She moaned. She couldn't run away from them. Even if she could make it through the woods to the parking lot, how would she get back home?

The howling grew sonorous[618].

Dina slowly opened her eyes, and they assimilated[619] to the darkness. Shapes and shadows moved. She had no way to escape. Falling to her knees, her body wracked with sobs, she gave in to them. This was the end of her. This was the end of everything she knew. She threw out her arms in supplication[620] to the dark figures who closed in on her and waited.

---

[615] Discord – lack of agreement or harmony

[616] Extinguished – put an end to, destroyed

[617] Aghast – struck by shock, terror or amazement

[618] Sonorous – having or producing a rich, deep sound

[619] Assimilated – adapted

[620] Supplication – plea, appeal, entreaty

CHAPTER THIRTEEN

"Dina!" Savannah vociferated[621] into the darkness. Trees surrounded her on all sides. Her flashlight gave off an anemic glow, barely lighting her way. She saw no path, only a tumble of underbrush and trees. Even if there were some clues to follow—a broken branch or a torn piece of clothing—she probably wouldn't have seen them in the darkness.

Gracelessly[622], she'd wandered the woods for fifteen minutes, tripping and stumbling. Her voice grew hoarse. "Dina!" Her scream cracked the dead air around her, echoing bleakly. She sounded so desperate, so frightened to her own ears. She had to find her friend. Now.

Up ahead she spied a weak, orange glow.

Could that be a fire? Could that be where Carter took her?

Savannah pushed through the branches. They tugged at her hair and tore at her clothes. One stubborn stick clawed her cheek, leaving a searing[623] scratch behind.

"Dina, I'm coming!" She had nothing with her—no weapon, not even her cell phone. She'd had no signal, but having her phone in her pocket would've made her feel marginally better. The civilized world felt so far away.

Savannah burst through the last line of trees into a small clearing. The fire smoldered. A few, weak flames licked at chunks

---

[621] Vociferated – uttered or cried loudly

[622] Gracelessly - clumsily

[623] Searing - burning

of charred wood. She'd stepped right into the middle of a weird circle, scratched into the dry earth. A pentagram. Just like the drawing in the notebook.

Involuntarily[624], she jumped out of the circle, as if it burned her. The quiet was absolute. No wind. No nocturnal[625] animals scurrying about. She shivered. Her flashlight quaked in her hand.

An enormous animal burst through the trees and knocked Savannah to the ground. The heavy weight of the animal's paws pinned her to the dirt. She screamed. Her flashlight tumbled into the fire and went out.

This was it. She was dead. She waited for the animal's razor-sharp claws to tear her to pieces. Whatever it was, she could see nothing but two glowing eyes. A bear? A wolf?

Fetid[626], warm breath emanated from the animal's mouth. Savannah turned her head away in disgust and fear.

The claws tensed, but did not penetrate her skin.

Why was this animal hesitating?

Savannah turned her head. Although she was horridly afraid, she sensed death hanging over her and wanted to confront[627] the nightmare that held her down. Why turn away from the inevitable[628]? Why be a coward now?

In the light of the full moon she could make out a snout, two pointed ears on a shaggy head, and—earrings?

What were earrings doing on an animal?

The wolf-like head tilted sideways. The glowing gaze studied her for a moment. The earrings jangled at the motion.

Those were Dina's earrings.

The creature snorted once and leapt off of her.

Savannah raised up on her elbows to get a closer look. Her fear converted[629] to curiosity.

The animal backed away from her with a strange limp in its right front paw, its long pink tongue hanging out of its mouth. It

---

[624] Involuntarily – not subject to the control of the volition

[625] Nocturnal – most active at night

[626] Fetid – having an offensive odor

[627] Confront – come face to face with

[628] Inevitable – impossible to avoid or prevent

[629] Converted – changed from one state or position to another

bounded into the woods leaving only a swirl of dust in its wake.

Savannah felt like she'd been punched in the stomach. She couldn't move for a long moment as she tried to process what had happened.

That was Dina.

Her friend was a werewolf incarnate[630]. Savannah could recognize those earrings from a mile away. She'd been too late to save her friend. The realization appalled[631] her.

Savannah crawled over to the dying fire. Her flashlight, now half charred, was useless. She pulled her knees to her chest. Tears welled in her eyes, and she cried at her failure to protect her friend. She cried because she was so alone and frightened. She cried in hopelessness. She and Nick barely knew anything about werewolves. Victims of their own temerity[632], they believed they could prevent something bad from happening to someone else.

Their naïve belief had been madness.

Savannah, adrenaline running high, knew she had to get back to her car. Who knew where the rest of the werewolves were? Maybe they were watching her right now. Maybe she was about to become their next victim.

She stumbled into the woods blindly. The moonlight barely penetrated the canopy of trees. She ran with her arms out in front of her, pushing through brambles and trees and bushes— oblivious[633] to the fact her clothes were being ripped to shreds.

She had to get to her car. She had to call Nick. He would be so fretful[634].

A symphony[635] of howls filled the woods around her.

They were after her.

Her breath came out in painful gasps. Her face was a crisscross of abrasions[636]. But she kept running—as if the devil was on her tail.

---

[630] Incarnate – embodied in human form

[631] Appalled – dismayed, alarmed

[632] Temerity – fearless daring

[633] Oblivious – lacking conscious awareness

[634] Fretful – marked by worry and distress

[635] Symphony – an orchestral concerts

[636] Abrasions – scraped areas on the skin

She could sense them right behind her. Any moment one of them would pounce on her, bring her down, rip her to pieces. Nick would never know what had happened to her. She burst through the trees and tumbled into the parking lot. She landed on her knees. Gravel scraped through her jeans and tore a hole. She pushed the pain aside, immersed in her escape.

The howling grew louder, closer.

Savannah wiped fresh tears from her face. Now she had tears of fear and dread, rather than sadness. She pulled out her keys and pressed the unlock button. Her car beeped reassuringly in response. She started her car with a loud thrum and looked over her shoulder to back out of the parking lot.

Ka-bang!

She whipped her head around. Her eyes widened in horror at the inimical[637] creature on the hood of her car. A huge, gray werewolf, teeth bared, stared at her through the windshield.

She screamed, punched the gas and spun the steering wheel. Her car reeled backwards, curving crazily on the gravel. The werewolf slipped off the hood, its claws scraping across the paint. As soon as she heard the thump of the werewolf landing on the ground, Savannah shifted quickly to drive and pressed down on the gas.

Tha-thump.

The car sickeningly bumped over the furry body on the ground. Savannah shuddered, but didn't look back. Maybe if she was lucky, she ran over its cranium[638]. She sped down the gravel road rife[639] with potholes. Twenty, thirty, forty miles an hour. Flying over one deep hole, her head slammed painfully against the ceiling of her car. The metallic tang of blood in her mouth made her realize she'd bitten her tongue.

"Dammit!" Her ailment[640] was more emotional than physical. Dina was lost to her and Nick. Savannah felt bereft[641]. Dina had

---

[637] Inimical – unfriendly or hostile

[638] Cranium – skull

[639] Rife – abundant or numerous

[640] Ailment – sickness, illness, complaint

[641] Bereft – sorrowful through loss or deprivation

become one of those abominable[642] werewolves. The tears coursed[643] down her cheeks. She'd failed her best friend.

Once she'd safely pulled onto the main road and had driven for several miles, she picked up her phone. She trembled as she hit redial.

Nick answered on the first ring. "Savannah! My God, are you all right?" He spoke with a zealousness[644] bordering on raving lunatic. "Where are you? I've been worried sick."

Savannah struggled to speak as calmly and clearly as she could. "They got Dina. They got her, Nick." Her voice grew thick with sorrow. "It's too late."

"You tell me where to meet you, and I'll be there." The depth of emotion in his voice scared her. He sounded beyond anger, beyond fear.

The clock on her dashboard read midnight. She'd been in the woods for almost ninety minutes. "I don't know."

"The school. Meet me in the parking lot."

"All right. I'll be there in ten minutes."

"I should get there before you do. If not, you keep your doors locked. Understand?"

"Yes."

"And Savannah?"

"Yes?" She shuddered but managed to keep her voice steady.

"It'll be okay. Everything's going to be okay."

Savannah hit the disconnect[645] button on her phone. How could Nick make everything okay? Dina had been turned. Her friend was now a monster like the other three, and they didn't know how to stop it from happening to someone else.

She drove her car like an automaton[646] and made the left turn at the 7-11. She stopped at the long red light near the dry cleaner's. Everything looked so normal and peaceful here in the center of town. The juxtaposition[647] of the horror in the woods and

---

[642] Abominable – detestable or loathsome

[643] Coursed – proceeded or moved quickly along a specified course

[644] Zealousness - eagerness

[645] Disconnect – sever or interrupt

[646] Automaton – one that behaves or responds in a mechanical way

[647] Juxtaposition – side-by-side position

the quiet of town startled her. No one in town knew what lurked only a few miles down the road. Teenagers were being targeted. Their lives were being destroyed. Werewolves were on the prowl and no one even knew.

She pulled into the school parking lot. Nick stood next to his car, tall and strong. A warm relief filled her. She finally felt safe.

*

"Savannah, you never should have gone to the woods alone," Nick reprimanded[648] her after he heard the details of what happened. He touched the scratches on her face with a gentle hand.

Savannah huddled in his car in her heavy sweater and coat, unable to get warm no matter how high Nick cranked up the heat. "I had to, Nick. Dina needed me. I could've saved her." She knew her distress must be palpable[649] in the close confines of the car.

"Don't blame yourself." Nick squeezed her hand reassuringly. "You couldn't have stopped this."

"We don't know that." She stared forlornly[650] out the window. Bright lights surrounded the parking lot. The phosphorescence[651] lit it up like an operating room.

"It's us against who knows how many. You said you saw Principal Morgan's car there." Nick dug for more information. "Did you ever see him?"

"No, but they were all changed." She shuddered at the memory of Dina in werewolf form looming over her, teeth gnashing[652] in the moonlight. "They were all those *things*..." She shivered at the lurid thought. The stoic[653], silver face of the moon shone through her window. Savannah remembered its light guiding her back to her car. The moon had been both friend to the werewolf and Savannah's savior. Strange to think that one object could be responsible for both things.

"Tomorrow, we're going to his office." A steely resolve

---

[648] Reprimanded – censure severely or angrily

[649] Palpable – easily perceived, obvious

[650] Forlornly – wretchedly, pitifully

[651] Phosphorescence – the property of emitting light

[652] Gnashing – grind or strike together

[653] Stoic –indifferent, impassive

settled in Nick's voice. "I'm tired of sneaking around, keeping this under wraps. I want to confront him about it."

"I don't know if that's such a good idea." She pulled out of his grasp.

"What's he going to do to me? Tear me to pieces right in his office?" The ire[654] in him boiled barely below the surface.

Nick was right. What could the principal possibly do in broad daylight amidst hundreds of high school kids and an office full of counselors and secretaries? She leveled her gaze at him and gritted her teeth. "You mean, what is he going to do to *us*. I'm going with you."

Nick raised his brows. "Are you sure you're up to that?"

"Dina's my best friend. I *have* to be involved." She hoped her umbrage[655] at his suggestion was apparent[656]. "I have to feel like I'm doing something for her."

Nick nodded.

Savannah knew he wanted to keep her far away from the werewolf menace[657], but he had to know that was impossible. There was no way she'd let him act alone. Dina was her friend, too. They had discovered this nightmare together. They both would pursue a solution together. Whatever that meant.

"Tomorrow, then." Nick said.

"Yeah, tomorrow." Savannah leaned her head against the window, wondering where Dina might be out in the dark, cold night. She hoped the other werewolves didn't hurt her.

Dina, we're coming for you. We're going to save you.

Savannah prayed they wouldn't be too late.

---

[654] Ire – anger, wrath

[655] Umbrage – offense or resentment

[656] Apparent – readily seen, visible

[657] Menace – possible danger, threat

CHAPTER FOURTEEN

Savannah should've known their plan would go awry[658] the moment they stepped into the principal's office to confront him. Savannah was shaking; Nick was seething[659]. Neither of them were thinking straight.

The secretary announced their arrival[660] over the intercom. Principal Morgan's voice came across gruff. "Send them in. They saved me the trouble of pulling them out of class."

Savannah's confidence drooped. The principal must know Savannah had been in the woods last night. The only thing she and Nick had going for them was surprise, and now that had been taken away.

Savannah clung to Nick. She reminded herself that nothing could happen to them in broad daylight. Before they opened the door to the principal's office Savannah caught a flash of intensity[661] in Nick's gaze. That flash made her certain he wouldn't let her down.

Principal Morgan sat behind his desk, a doleful[662] look clouded his face. "I've decided that you two are going to help me."

His words caught them off guard. This was what not they'd expected to hear. Savannah stood mutely. She didn't know if she

---

[658] Awry – away from the corrected course
[659] Seething – violently excited or agitated
[660] Arrival – the act of arriving, entering
[661] Intensity – exceptionally great concentration, power or force
[662] Doleful – filled with or evoking sadness

should turn around and run or sit down and listen to what the man had to say.

She slid weak-kneed[663] into an empty chair. Would he tell them they were next? That there was no hope? That they might as well give up and join the werewolves?

"Help you?" Savannah wished she felt more secure with Nick standing right behind her. He might only be seventeen, but he stood over six feet tall—almost matching the principal's height. However, what would height accomplish[664] in an uneven match? What had happened to Dina had been a supernatural[665] event. If the principal was one of them, they weren't dealing with a typical[666] human.

"I've been trying to keep this quiet since the beginning of the school year." The principal's demeanor was relaxed. Not exactly the stance an attacking werewolf would take. "I didn't want to panic the parents, and I certainly didn't want to bring the media in here scaring all the students. But it seems like you two have figured this out on your own, and I can't allow it to go any further."

What was he talking about? Could it be that they were wrong? Maybe the principal wasn't involved at all.

"But you were there last night." Savannah needed an explanation. "In the woods. You mean to tell me that you aren't one of them? One of those—werewolves?"

To hear the word 'werewolf' said aloud made Savannah's feel delirious[667].

"What?" The principal widen his eyes at her statement. "Me?" He chortled. "I've been trying to stop this since the beginning. Since you and your ace researcher here couldn't keep your noses out of it, I might as well take you under my wing. I'd rather keep an eye on you than let you end up massacred[668]."

An hysterical[669] laugh threatened to burst out of her mouth.

---

[663] Weak-kneed – lacking strength of character or purpose

[664] Accomplish – succeed in doing

[665] Supernatural – caused by a power that violates natural forces

[666] Typical – conforming to a type

[667] Delirious - hallucinating

[668] Massacred – killed indiscriminately, slaughtered

[669] Hysterically – marked by excessive or uncontrollable emotion

The principal of her high school wanted to stop someone's depraved[670] plan to turn students into werewolves. The whole situation sounded so ludicrous. The secret had been one between her and her friends. Never in a million years did she think she'd be having this discussion with her principal. She took a breath to calm herself and move forward on how they were going to work together to end this. The ridiculousness could wait for another day.

Savannah directed the conversation back to last night. "So how did you end up out in the woods?"

"I was doing some recon, scoping out the area, getting a handle on the problem. Then you showed up."

"I had to save her." Who cared if she got in the way of his 'recon'? Dina had needed her help. She wouldn't have done anything differently even if she knew why the principal's car had been parked there.

Principal Morgan waved his hand at her. "Look, you're two smart kids. You almost had it figured out before I did. That stuff in the woods was the nail in the coffin as far as I'm concerned."

"Nail in the coffin?" Nick inquired[671].

"Yes. I've hired someone to take care of the problem. A werewolf hunter. But I need some inside knowledge to know how you teenage kids think—where you like to hang out and whom you like to hang out with. Now, I've been doing some research, as an antecedent[672] to any actions…"

"That was *your* notebook we found, wasn't it?" Nick crossed his arms.

The principal relaxed his tight jaw. "It *was* you. I thought so." He snapped his fingers. "I was worried that it had been…"

The door creaked open. Savannah jumped at the noise.

"Here's our hunter now. Perfect timing." Principal Morgan put his feet up on his desk and tucked his hands behind his head.

"Here *who* is now?" Nick queried[673], echoing Savannah's own thoughts.

"Daniel. Daniel the Werewolf Hunter. I found an ad in an

---

[670] Depraved – morally corrupt, perverted

[671] Inquired - asked

[672] Antecedent – a preceding occurrence or event

[673] Queried - questioned

old copy of *Arms and Ammo* magazine at the library." He gave a satisfied smile. "He came highly recommended."

Savannah wanted to ask where someone goes for a recommendation on a werewolf hunter, but she was silenced when the specter[674] of a tall figure appeared.

"Frank, good to see you again." A well-built man in a dark trench coat and a black fedora hat entered. He reached out a meaty hand to give the principal a cordial[675] handshake. "Glad you decided to take me up on my offer. Some may consider my prices extortionate[676], but I'm sure you've heard that I'm worth every penny."

"That I did, Daniel. That I did." Principal Morgan leaned back comfortably in his padded chair. He gestured[677] at Nick and Savannah. "These are the two I was telling you about last night."

"Great." Daniel had overly-long brown hair that stuck out from underneath his hat. He nodded at them and set down a backpack that looked replete[678] with something.

What did he have in there? Silver bullets? Wooden stakes and crucifixes? Or did those only work on vampires?

Savannah couldn't believe her principal had hired a stranger out of a magazine. Daniel looked as if he'd just stepped off the set for an action film.

Was this guy for real?

"All right, kids, this is the game plan." Daniel took control of the meeting, swaggering back and forth in the small office. The fact they were high school kids didn't seem to bother him at all. "We do some training—after school when possible. Then, we scout out locations for hopeful interactions with the subjects."

"Training?" Nick looked askance[679].

"Target practice, evasive maneuvers[680], werewolf anatomy[681],

---

[674] Specter – a ghostly appearing figure

[675] Cordial – warm and sincere, friendly

[676] Extortionate – exorbitant, immoderate

[677] Gestured – moved the limbs or body for emphasis

[678] Replete - filled

[679] Askance – with disapproval, suspicion or disgust

[680] Maneuvers – movements involving skill or dexterity

[681] Anatomy – bodily structure of an animal or plant

and so forth."

Nick nodded his head as if this all made logical sense. Savannah had been stunned into muteness.

What kind of evasive maneuvers did he mean? Was she expected to take on a werewolf all by herself? And what about saving Dina? This sounded like an all-out assault, not a rescue operation.

Daniel must have noticed her shocked face, but chose to ignore it. He plowed on with his oratory[682]. "As I was saying, we do recon, root out hiding places and gathering areas, et cetera. We take down the subjects one by one, and hopefully eliminate[683] the master werewolf."

"The master?" Nick appeared to be warming up to the idea of taking on a band of bloodthirsty, supernatural beings.

Savannah wanted to cower in a corner, but Nick's interest grew with each horrifying detail. He was a teenage boy running high on adrenaline and testosterone, Savannah supposed.

"Yes, a werewolf clan[684]. We'll be covering this in the history portion so no need to take notes."

Centerville was a Podunk town where nothing ever happened. Who would've targeted their town for a werewolf invasion?

Daniel continued. "A clan is made up of two parts: the master and his slaves. Our ultimate goal is to locate the master. If we destroy him, we may be able to save the slaves."

Savannah perked up her ears. "There's a chance to save them?"

"A slave who has not tasted human blood has a small window of opportunity for reversion[685]. Note I said, 'small.' We aren't here to be heroes. We aren't here to save lives. We're here to prevent an epidemic[686]. It's important that we look at these werewolves, some of whom may be family or friends, as nothing more than carriers of a deadly disease. The only way to break the

---

[682] Oratory – speech, address

[683] Eliminate – get rid of, remove

[684] Clan – a large group of friends, relatives or associates

[685] Reversion – a return to a former condition, belief or interest

[686] Epidemic – an outbreak of a disease that spreads rapidly

cycle of disease is to take out the infected."

Principal Morgan took up the charge. "Do you see now why I kept everything so quiet? It's an epidemic. And an epidemic of these proportions would only instigate[687] panic. I can't have chaos[688] in my school."

Savannah wanted to point out that Jenna and Dina had suffered plenty due to his worries about inciting panic, but she bit her tongue. She couldn't do anything about what had happened at the school. She should turn her focus to saving her friend rather than trying to understand how this all began. Dina would've done the same for her if their roles were reversed.

"When do we start?" she asked definitively[689]. She pushed aside any qualms[690] she had about involving herself in something so dangerous. Dina's life was at stake.

Daniel gave her a toothy grin and slapped her on the back. "That's what I need—enthusiasm, resolve, fortitude. Mr. Morgan, you've chosen wisely. Very wise choices indeed."

Nick gave Savannah's hand a comforting squeeze. Savannah squeezed back, but couldn't help feeling she was getting in way over her head.

*

"The history of the werewolf has many gaps. Working from a few surviving texts from the Dark Ages, we aren't quite clear on the origins of werewolves, but we have learned a few important facts." Daniel the Werewolf Hunter lectured to Savannah and Nick from the back of his panel van, which was an inglorious[691] location for learning. From the outside, the van appeared to be abandoned in an empty lot next to the school's athletic fields. It suited their purpose, however. Where else could they discuss werewolves in secret?

Instead of preparing for the Homecoming Dance, Nick and Savannah sat through the most eccentric[692] lecture of their lives.

---

[687] Instigate – stir up, foment

[688] Chaos – a condition of great disorder or confusion

[689] Definitively – authoritatively

[690] Qualms – uneasiness, misgivings

[691] Inglorious - disgraceful

[692] Eccentric – odd or unconventional

They sat side by side on the shaggy orange carpet, which covered the entire van from floor to ceiling.

Savannah wondered why Daniel chose this particular vehicle as his main mode of transportation and command central. It looked like the fantasy of some sixteen-year-old boy from 1975. Savannah tried to disregard[693] the nausea-inducing carpet color and concentrate on taking notes.

"Fact number one, werewolves are not immortal[694]. They can be killed quite easily when the correct implements[695] are used." Daniel pulled a .45 from a duffle bag and pointed it up at the ceiling. "A silver bullet is the best method, but any weapon of pure silver that can perforate[696] the body can also be used." He showed them an arrow with a silver tip, a pair of scissors, and a long-bladed hunting knife.

Savannah shivered as she imagined using one of the weapons he displayed.

"There's no need to worry." Daniel slid each silver item back into the bag. "I'll be in charge of the weapons here. I don't expect either of you to get involved in the actual kills. I do think it's necessary, however, that you know all the details for your own safety. Fact number two, only a master werewolf can create slave werewolves. If we can find the master werewolf, killing the slaves should be a facile[697] job."

"I thought you said we could save the slaves." Savannah's gut clenched at Daniel's words.

Was there no hope for Dina?

"Ah, yes, I'd forgotten one of the slaves is a good friend of yours." Daniel cracked his knuckles. "There's a chance she can be saved—a slight chance—if we find her before she tastes human blood. How long has she been missing?"

"Since last night."

"The process of becoming a werewolf is threefold," Daniel

---

[693] Disregard – ignore

[694] Immortal – everlasting, not subject to death

[695] Implements – tools or instruments

[696] Perforate – pierce, penetrate

[697] Facile – easy, effortless

enumerated[698]. "First, one must be bitten by a master werewolf on the night of a full moon; two, for three days one must be kept in almost complete darkness to experience transformation; three, one must feed on human flesh. If all three of these criteria[699] are met, a new werewolf is created."

Savannah's stomach turned at the grotesque[700] thought of her friend dining on a human being. "Will she be aware of what she used to be?"

"I don't usually take the time to have a conversation with 'em." Daniel gave a callous[701] shrug.

"So, are you saying that you never returned a werewolf to human form?" Nick clenched his fists.

Savannah was equally upset. If Daniel the Werewolf Hunter couldn't help them with all of his erudition[702] about werewolves, than what were they doing in this squalid[703] old van anyway? Yes, they wanted to stop the werewolves from spreading, but their main mission was to save their friend. To Savannah, it seemed this Daniel person couldn't care less about Dina.

"Look, I was hired for one purpose—to get rid of the werewolf infestation[704]. You're going to help me." Daniel narrowed his eyes at them. "If—and this is a big if—*if* we have a chance to seize[705] this Dina person, I'll do what I can, but there are no guarantees."

Anger welled up inside her. Principal Morgan had brought in Daniel as the clean up man, not as the rescuer. She and Nick would have to be the ones to make sure Dina survived. They'd better stick like glue to Daniel to make sure it happened.

"Now, if there aren't any further questions, I think we've covered enough ground for one day." Daniel placed his cache of weapons behind him. "We've got a lot to do before tonight. We'll

---

[698] Enumerated – count off, name one by one
[699] Criteria – standard or rule on which a decision can be based
[700] Grotesque – distorted, abnormal, hideous
[701] Callous – emotionally hardened, unfeeling
[702] Erudition – deep, extensive learning
[703] Squalid – foul, run-down, repulsive
[704] Infestation – the state of being overrun by parasites
[705] Seize – take into custody, capture

meet here at midnight. Principal Morgan will play his role during the Homecoming Dance, and we do the rest."

Daniel's plan entailed searching at the school and branching outward. Although Nick had proposed the woods as a better starting point, Daniel posited[706] that someone in the school had to be involved. Principal Morgan seemed sure a faculty member had a hand in what was going on.

Savannah was scared, but Nick's resolve helped her feel stronger. They were doing this for Dina, she reminded herself. How she wished she could just carry on her normal, scholarly[707] life and forget all this werewolf nonsense, but she couldn't turn back now.

---

[706] Posited – put forward, as for consideration or study
[707] Scholarly – intellectual, characteristic of a studious person

CHAPTER FIFTEEN

"You did well at the ceremony. Our newest recruit will join us soon." The head werewolf surveyed her pack gathered in the school's basement. "We will need to find a new den that is dark, invulnerable[708] and quiet before we recruit again." A faint mewling escaped into the corridor of the high school basement. The girl had awoken. "Go to her." The Master pointed a needle-sharp claw at Jenna.

Jenna withdrew from the ranks and slipped inside the dark holding cell.

Jenna's loyalty was absolute[709]. Fascinating how quickly the recruits allowed their individuality to atrophy[710] and embraced the structured, narrow life of a werewolf slave.

The Master reveled in her powers as Master Werewolf. She'd progressed from powerless to powerful in such a short period of time. Her new status was as addictive as any narcotic.

She remembered her former life as a weak and fragile human. Painful memories of childhood vexed[711] her. Her nights had been spent locked in a closet, her days nothing but a series of beatings and isolation[712]. Her parents had been her jailers, barely tolerating her presence. Somehow she'd survived. She'd managed

---

[708] Invulnerable – immune to attack, impregnable

[709] Absolute – complete, unconditional

[710] Atrophy – to cause to wither or deteriorate

[711] Vexed – irritated, distressed

[712] Isolation – setting something apart from others

to make it to adulthood. At eighteen she'd swore never to be impotent[713] again and never to be intimidated by another human being.

That one ambition[714] took her on a ten-year journey. Years of research and failed attempts to find the right solution. Martial arts classes, weight-lifting, gun training. When those didn't work and human pursuits left her unfulfilled, she moved on to the occult.

She'd traveled many black and horrific paths until she found the solution. Finding that big red book had been preordained[715]. She found in its pages everything she'd been searching for.

The werewolf had been the perfect choice: preternaturally strong, swift, and feared by man for centuries. Her research revealed, if the transformation was completed in the right way, she could become the leader of a pack of slave werewolves, making her almost invincible[716].

To transform had been much easier than she'd imagined. One night in the woods, during a full moon, she'd killed another master werewolf. The gun had been loaded with silver bullets. The werewolf had been poised to devour her; she only needed it to bite her. Timing had been vital[717] to avoid a fatal bite. First, she'd needed one bite from the werewolf, then she'd needed to kill. No mistakes, no second chances.

The bite in her thigh had been dolorous[718], but killing the werewolf had been the most powerful, most visceral moment of her life. With one sure-aimed bullet to the skull, the werewolf had gone down. Immediately, she was imbued[719] with astonishing strength and confidence.

Without someone to instruct her, however, she'd struggled those first few years to understand her new self. Controlling and honing her abilities took many months of practice.

---

[713] Impotent – lacking physical strength or vigor, weak

[714] Ambition – an eager or strong desire to achieve something

[715] Preordained – determined beforehand

[716] Invincible – incapable of being overcome or defeated

[717] Vital – urgently needed, absolutely necessary

[718] Dolorous – marked by or exhibiting pain, grief or sorrow

[719] Imbued – permeated, saturated

This summer she'd decided to create and subjugate[720] new werewolves as her slaves. The red book had been her guide. These slaves would be her army who would surround and protect her, so her life was never endangered[721] again.

A howl erupted from the room that held the newest slave. This girl would soon learn her place. Once the transformation was complete, the slave would forget her old self. The Master smiled. Her plan was coming together. On the next full moon, they would be able to take two more recruits—the girl's friends. They'd gotten too close to the truth. What better way to take care of them than to make them werewolves?

The Master slunk along the cobwebbed corridors beneath the school, leaving Jenna to teach Dina the ways of the werewolf. The Master didn't need to be here for the process. Besides, she was hungry, and it was time to hunt.

*

The high school was abnormally[722] quiet for Homecoming. Nick, Savannah, and Daniel sat in the dilapidated[723] van and watched the low-lying building for signs of movement. An hour had passed, and so far they'd only observed a few stragglers from the dance.

For a moment, Savannah wished that werewolves and Dina's disappearance were only part of a bad dream. Savannah wanted to be one of those oblivious[724] students. A spaghetti-strap blue dress hung in Savannah's closet at home. She was supposed to be wearing that dress tonight. Her heart ached for what should've been. Savannah was cognizant of the fact she and Nick should've been enjoying their Friday evening together. Their first date.

How did they end up in this smelly, garish[725] van with Daniel the weirdo?

Daniel hunkered down and polished his glossy crossbow with its 99.9% pure silver arrow tip sticking out.

---

[720] Subjugate – make subservient, enslave

[721] Endangered – exposed to harm or danger, imperiled

[722] Abnormally – unusually

[723] Dilapidated – having fallen into a state of deterioration

[724] Oblivious – lacking conscious awareness of

[725] Garish – tastelessly showy, gaudy

Savannah's patience wore thin. "Aren't we supposed to be doing more than just sitting here?" At least three werewolves were holding Dina captive somewhere. She couldn't believe Daniel spent the last few hours sitting in a van reading magazines, casing the school with his binoculars, and cleaning weapons. She wanted to be out there looking for her friend. This was a waste of time.

Daniel focused on his crossbow and slid an <u>unctuous</u>[726] cloth up and down the stock of the weapon. "We will. Shortly."

Nick's gaze hardened to steel. "Well, I'm getting out of here. Dina's in trouble," Nick said <u>fervently</u>[727]. "If she's here, I want to find her."

Before Daniel could set down the crossbow, Nick headed out the back door and pulled Savannah with him. "We don't need this guy. We can do this ourselves." He was <u>fractious</u>[728].

Savannah's heart leapt at the determination in Nick's voice. He'd grown tired of listening to lectures and being ordered around, too. The two of them had started this on their own, and they could finish it on their own.

"I'm responsible for you," Daniel yelled after them. He tripped over his duffle bag and stumbled out of the van. "Get back here! You don't know what you're doing! You're going to get yourselves killed!"

Savannah was <u>amenable</u>[729] to Nick leading the charge. He had as much concern for Dina as she did. Daniel, however, didn't think their friend was worth saving.

She looked over her shoulder at the shelter they were leaving behind. Daniel lugged his crossbow and his duffle bag loaded with weaponry. He was hot on their tail.

Maybe they should stick together. Maybe that would be the safer thing to do.

Savannah vacillated, but let Nick lead her toward the school. The gravity of the situation bogged her down. She had no idea what the best move would be. Stick with Nick? Or wait for Daniel to catch up?

---

[726] Unctuous - oily

[727] Fervently – with passionate feeling

[728] Fractious – having a peevish nature, cranky

[729] Amenable - willing

They reached the cafeteria. Nick pushed on each set of doors. Miraculously, one door swung open.

Savannah's thoughts coalesced. Her nerves were ripped to shreds. She searched for werewolves out here, unprotected. Split up their little group would not be as efficacious[730]. Abetting[731] Nick in his two-man crusade tempted her, but she felt it was not the smartest choice. She didn't like Daniel ordering them around, but at least he had guns and knives and crossbows. She stopped in her tracks at the door and abstained[732] from going any further.

Nick balked[733] at her resistance, and his eyes clouded over. "So, you're gonna choose that nut over me? I just want to find Dina, Savannah. Can't you do this for me?"

"I can't." She shook her head, and tears spilled down her face. She couldn't force herself through the cafeteria door and into the unknown. Not even if Nick were by her side.

He held the door open for a moment, as if he hoped she would change her mind. His blue gaze burned into hers, a silent plea[734] to come with him. When she didn't, his mouth set in a restive[735] line. He let go of the door. A pained expression darkened his features for a moment. He let the door shut in her face.

As soon as Nick was gone, Savannah felt loss and emptiness. She'd let her fear get the best of her. How could she do that to him? Would he forgive her? Her weakness disgusted her.

Daniel had caught up to her. He pulled her roughly away from the door. "Are you guys obtuse[736]? What were you thinking?" He gestured at the door Nick had entered. "That idiot is going to get himself killed!" He grabbed two thin-bladed knives from his duffle bag and handed them to her. "Here, take these. You said you've never had any gun training, right?" He pierced her with his fierce gaze. The brim of his fedora darkened his face. The harsh parking lot lights threw sharp shadows across everything.

---

[730] Efficacious – effective, producing an intended result

[731] Abetting – urging, encouraging, helping

[732] Abstained – refrained from something by one's own choice

[733] Balked – refused obstinately or abruptly

[734] Plea – earnest request, appeal

[735] Restive - tense

[736] Obtuse – lacking intellectual acuity

She took the knives from his grasp. Sweat made her hands clammy. A quick movement behind Daniel caught her attention. "Daniel?"

As if he had a sixth sense, Daniel <u>deftly</u>[737] spun in a smooth arc, trench coat flaring out behind him. He snapped the crossbow up to his eye, finger on the catch.

"Get inside," he <u>exhorted</u>[738]. "Now!"

Savannah slammed into the door and flung it violently inward. The string twanged on the bow. She scurried into the dimly-lit cafeteria. Her heart pounded like thunder in her chest.

Before the door could shut behind her, Daniel skidded through. "Move it!" he <u>goaded</u>[739] and shoved her toward the doors at the other end of the <u>commodious</u>[740] room.

Savannah lost her footing and almost dropped the knives in her grip. She ran to the exit doors that led to the inner hallway. She had no time to think. No time to wonder if Daniel's arrow hit its mark. She dashed through the empty cafeteria and hoped to see Nick. He'd only entered a few seconds ahead of them. The darkness <u>inhibited</u>[741] her. She could only make out the shadowy outlines of folded tables. She reached the exit doors.

"Get down!" Daniel rushed up behind her and pushed her to the floor. He dropped his duffle bag, reloaded his crossbow with another arrow, and aimed.

Thwack.

Savannah scrambled behind a folded-up cafeteria table. She braced for a yelp from the werewolf target, but heard only the clatter of the arrow as it missed its mark.

Daniel <u>blasphemed</u>[742] under his breath and reached for his bag. His <u>profile</u>[743] was barely visible in the <u>somberness</u>[744].

Savannah heard the unmistakable clacking of claws on tile

---

[737] Deftly – quickly and skillfully

[738] Exhorted – urged by strong admonition or appeal

[739] Goaded – incited, roused

[740] Commodious – roomy, spacious

[741] Inhibited – restrained, prevented

[742] Blasphemed – uttered obscenities or profanities

[743] Profile – a side view of an object or structure

[744] Somberness – state of partial or total darkness

and a deep growl.

Daniel pulled a revolver from his bag and prepared to aim. A dark blur of fur and claws knocked him to the ground.

Savannah screamed and scrabbled toward the exit doors. A huge gray werewolf pinned Daniel to the floor. Daniel swung his gun toward the creature, but the werewolf clamped down on his arm. Incisors[745] crunched though ligament[746] and bone. Blood spurted from the bite. Daniel gave a primal scream. The werewolf snarled and wrenched its muscular neck from right to left. Savannah thought Daniel's arm would be torn from its socket.

Bewildered[747] and horrified by the turn of events, Savannah scrambled to her feet to escape. Daniel's strangled cry stopped her.

She gripped the sharp, silver knives as if they were lifelines. Now, they were the only things that would save her and Daniel. A surge of adrenaline suppressed[748] her flight response. She flicked the long, pointed blades outward, one in each hand, and leapt at the werewolf. An angry growl of odium[749] burst from her throat, and she thrust the knives forward, jabbing at the furry body with all her might.

The blades sunk in to the flesh with a sickening, wet slide. The werewolf gave a torturous[750] grunt, twisting its body in a writhing[751] motion. It released Daniel's arm, and blood streamed from its mouth.

Savannah shuddered at the grisly[752] sight. She poised[753] ready to strike again. The werewolf rose up. Panic coiled in her stomach, and she backed up against the wall. For a brief moment, the werewolf moved toward her, but then fell onto its back. A huge shuddering breath rattled in its chest, and the werewolf went still.

"Daniel." The sight of all the blood and the exposed wound

---

[745] Incisors – a tooth for cutting or gnawing

[746] Ligament – sheet of tough fibrous tissues connecting bones

[747] Bewildered – confused or befuddled

[748] Suppressed – put down by force or authority

[749] Odium – strong dislike, contempt or aversion

[750] Torturous – extremely painful, agonizing

[751] Writhing – twisting in pain

[752] Grisly – shockingly repellant, inspiring horror

[753] Poised – held in suspension, hovered

made her sick to her stomach. The bite was severe. Blood poured from the jagged tear of flesh, which extended from his upper arm all the way down to his wrist.

Daniel's eyes fluttered. His achromatic[754] face was the color of death.

Savannah had no way to staunch the flow of blood. She pressed her hands to his arm. Blood flowed freely between her fingers, forming a pool on the tile floor.

"Daniel, wake up! You have to help me. I don't know what to do." Tears ran down her face. She avoided looking at the shaggy body lying only a few feet from Daniel. She'd killed that thing, and there were more where that one came from.

Daniel shook violently for a few seconds and tried to speak. His mouth opened and closed like a fish, but no sound came out. Savannah bent over him and held onto his unaffected[755] hand. She prayed he would survive. Her cell phone had been left behind in the van when Nick had pulled her out. She had no way to get help.

Daniel stopped shaking. His gaze, which once had been so piercing, now focused blindly up at the ceiling. He was dead.

She wiped the coagulating[756] blood on her jeans and snatched up the duffle bag. She pried the gun from Daniel's hand and ran out into the hallway. She needed to find a place to hide where she could think things through.

Where was Nick? Where could he have gone?

She regretted not following Nick into the cafeteria. Daniel's experience had done nothing for him. Daniel might have had the knowledge about how to kill werewolves, but the creature had been so big, so strong, so swift. He would've been better off relying on instinct. She'd be lucky to succeed in killing another one on her own. She needed to find Nick before the werewolves did.

The possibility of Nick dying like Daniel made her ill. She visualized[757] Daniel's ruined body as she made her way down the hall. Her knees wobbled. She needed to push the image from her mind or she'd end up a useless heap on the floor. She took a deep

---

[754] Achromatic – having no color, colorless

[755] Unaffected – not changed or modified

[756] Coagulating – changing from a liquid to a thickened state

[757] Visualized – formed a mental image

breath and struggled to gain control. A hunter must be prepared. *Think like a hunter.*

Savannah rooted around in the duffle bag and pulled out a jagged hunting knife. Her hand also touched the cold metal of Daniel's pistol. The gun was probably the better choice, but she was a novice[758] when it came to firearms. She tucked the twelve-inch blade in the back of her pants and left the gun in the bag. Having the knife made her more placid[759]. Knowing she had some kind of protection from the werewolves gave her a spurt of optimism[760]. She could find Nick. They could do this together.

Daniel had taught them quite a bit. Maybe they weren't werewolf experts, but they had enough information to eradicate[761] the master werewolf and save Dina. Daniel had given the impression it would be simple. She clung to that hope. To think otherwise would undermine her new frame of mind. She was strong. She was tough. She could do this.

Savannah slung the heavy bag over her shoulder and crept along the hallway. She stuck close to the lockers.

Where would Nick have gone? The classrooms? The library?

Daniel had said they needed to find the den—a gathering place where they would keep Dina until she'd completed the change from human to werewolf. Somewhere dark. Somewhere out of the way. Somewhere that wouldn't be noticed.

Where in the school building could you hide a pack of werewolves?

The only dark, desolate spot she could think of was the basement. The P.E. teachers stored old sports equipment down there, and the janitor kept a significant[762] supply of cleaning products and paper towels. That had to be where Nick was headed.

She moved toward the service door at the termination[763] of the building. The glare from the football field through the glass doors provided her only light. She tiptoed along and made sure nothing followed her. She caught a flash of movement and

---

[758] Novice - beginner

[759] Placid – calm, quiet

[760] Optimism – a tendency to expect the best possible outcome

[761] Eradicate – destroy completely

[762] Significant – fairly large in amount or quantity

[763] Termination – place where something ends

snapped her focus toward it. The hairs prickled[764] on the back of her neck and her heart fluttered like a wild bird against the bars of its cage. She froze. Inch by inch, she reached for the hilt of the hunting knife.

---

[764] Prickled – rose or stood up like prickles

CHAPTER SIXTEEN

"Savannah?" Nick whispered gruffly. "Is that you?"

Savannah let go of the knife hilt. Euphoria[765] slammed into her.

Nick.

She let the heavy bag slip off her shoulder and reached out for him. "Thank God, Nick." No longer alone, the adrenaline that had been pushing her, dissipated[766]. She slumped against the lockers.

He caught her up in his arms and enveloped her in a warm embrace. She leaned into his body and found much needed strength there.

"Are you all right?" he whispered into her hair. He gave her a quick assessment[767], searching for injuries. He touched her pants leg, which was tacky with werewolf blood. "Where's Daniel?"

Horror permeated[768] every fiber of her being when she heard Daniel's name. Savannah didn't have the energy to explain the deadly altercation[769] between Daniel and the werewolf. "Come on. We have to keep moving. They'll find us if we don't." They had no

---

[765] Euphoria – a feeling of great happiness or well-being

[766] Dissipated – vanished, disappeared

[767] Assessment – the act of judging or assessing a person or situation

[768] Permeated – spread or flowed throughout

[769] Altercation – noisy quarrel

time for a consensus[770] about their next move. She tugged him toward the basement access door.

"Whose blood is that? Did you see one of them?" He perused[771] her features for the answer to his question. "Did you?" His jaw tightened.

"Yes." A pain stabbed her heart at the incontrovertible[772] truth. "Daniel's dead. I had to kill that *thing*." She stared down the hall. She could envision the creature sprawled out in front of her. "It's in the cafeteria."

"You killed it?" Nick didn't seem to believe Savannah could be so intrepid[773].

Savannah couldn't believe her strength either. In her mind's eye, someone else had killed that werewolf. Only the blood on her jeans told her otherwise. "I think Dina—and the rest of them—might be in the basement. We're going to have to do this ourselves, Nick."

Nick grabbed the duffle bag from her and pulled out the gun. Daniel's blood stained the butt of it—a portent[774] of what was to come. Nick wiped it on his t-shirt. "Let's go."

They headed toward the basement access door. Nick took the lead, gun pointed and ready to fire. Savannah pulled up the rear and made sure to keep an eye on the empty hallway behind her.

The audible[775] click of claws on tile broke the silence. From the shadows of the stairwell, two bristling[776], shaggy bodies slunk toward them, growling.

"Get behind me." Nick pushed Savannah against the lockers and compelled[777] her to remain there. He aimed the revolver at the werewolves. The creatures crept forward by small increments[778]. The weapon pointed in their direction didn't even faze them.

---

[770] Consensus – general agreement

[771] Perused – read or examined with great care

[772] Incontrovertible – impossible to dispute

[773] Intrepid – courageous, fearless

[774] Portent – indication of something important about to occur

[775] Audible – that is heard or can be heard

[776] Bristling – raising the bristles

[777] Compelled – drove, forced

[778] Increments – something added or gained

Nick fired. An ear-splitting blast echoed through the empty corridor. Savannah flinched, but fixed her gaze on the werewolves. The larger werewolf snapped its head back as if it had been hit with a load of bricks. It fell to the floor with a shudder, and a pool of dark blood formed under its shaggy head.

Who knew a science nerd could be such a crack shot?

Nick, with the right impetus[779], had an innate[780] talent for guns.

The other werewolf disappeared like a wisp of smoke. Nick didn't have time to take aim again, but he fired succinctly[781] a few more times into the blackness.

Savannah hoped he got lucky and hit the second target. Her grip tightened on the hunting knife. She didn't want to use it, but was prepared if she had to. The darkness swallowed the other werewolf. Neither of them relaxed. They knew it would be back.

Nick tucked the gun in his pants and picked up the duffle bag. "Come on. Let's go." He headed through the basement access door without even a glance back at the still, furry body on the floor.

The plenitude[782] of darkness inside the doorway made Savannah feel claustrophobic. "We can't go down there without a flashlight."

A pathetic whimpering echoed up from the bowels of the school.

Dina.

She was down there somewhere. They had to help her.

"There must be a light switch around here," Nick said.

With a bit of serendipity[783], Nick must've found a switch. A fluorescent light flickered on at the bottom of the stairs. Although it appeared to be a characteristic[784] basement, Savannah imagined they were entering the depths of the underworld[785]. She and Nick

---

[779] Impetus – something that incites, stimulus

[780] Innate – not established by conditioning or learning

[781] Succinctly – with concise and precise brevity

[782] Plenitude – abundance

[783] Serendipity – the instance of making a fortunate discovery

[784] Characteristic - typical

[785] Underworld – the world of the dead, hell

had managed to kill two werewolves—both of them probably former acquaintances[786] at school. They had two more to tackle, one of which was the head werewolf. Daniel had told them unambiguously[787] that the master werewolf would not risk itself unless it had no choice.

"Come on." Nick took the steep concrete steps two at a time.

Savannah tried to keep up. The basement was a maze of pipes, ductwork, and cardboard boxes. As they moved along, they tried every door they came across. Most were locked, so they listened against the metal panels for any sounds of distress. When they reached the last few doors, tension emerged[788] from her body. Dina had to be in one of these rooms. It was eerily quiet. The whimpers and growling had ceased.

Nick turned the knob of the first door. It gave, and he swung it open. Savannah stood behind him. Her nerves were raw. In the corner, heavy, iron trammels[789] lay on top of a worn and stained mattress. An overpowering, putrid aroma[790] hung heavily in the stuffy room, assailing[791] her nose. Savannah backed away in disgust.

"She was here." Savannah knew without a doubt this is where they'd held Dina after she'd been abducted[792]. They were too late. She was gone. The werewolves must have moved her only minutes earlier.

Nick swore and slammed his fist into the metal door with a bang. "Where did those monstrosities[793] take her?" His words echoed Savannah's thoughts.

"There has to be another way out of the basement." Savannah was determined not to give up now. They were so close. "Let's go."

---

[786] Acquaintances – persons whom one knows

[787] Unambiguously – clearly

[788] Emerged – came out of

[789] Trammels – a restraint or shackles

[790] Aroma – a quality that can be perceived by the olfactory sense

[791] Assailing – attacking or assaulting

[792] Abducted – carried off by force, kidnapped

[793] Monstrosities – something hideous or frightful

Nick nodded. They headed to the end of the building and hit a concrete wall. No second set of steps. No hidden door.

How could they have disappeared?

"We had them." Nick's reservoir[794] of patience sounded almost empty. "We had them cornered."

"There must be another way out of this place." Savannah tucked the hunting knife back in the waistband of her pants. "Could they have sneaked past us when we came from the stairs?"

"I don't see how. It's pretty cramped down here." Nick scanned the tangle of pipes above their heads. "What about a window? Or some kind of secret passage?"

"Let's check out the room where they hid her. Maybe there'll be a clue." The werewolves were cunning[795], but they couldn't have disappeared without leaving a trace behind somewhere. They entered the secluded[796] cell where Dina had been for the last twenty-four hours. The fluorescent fixtures in the basement hallway provided their only light.

"Is there a light in here?" Savannah groped along the wall and found a switch. "Got it."

A single, bare bulb lit up the dingy room.

Nick lifted up the mattress and checked every corner for some trace of the werewolves or Dina. She and Nick were indefatigable[797] in their search. Nick spied a ceiling tile set slightly crooked. This was the only room with a drop ceiling anywhere in the basement. Nick bumped the tile with his hand and pushed it aside.

"They went this way." Nick scrutinized the exposed ceiling.

Someone had carefully chipped away at the concrete floor of the school above them and dissembled[798] a trapdoor there.

"Where do you think it goes?" Savannah prayed Dina was on the other side of the trapdoor.

"Only one way to find out." Nick grabbed a rickety wooden

---

[794] Reservoir – extra supply or reserve

[795] Cunning – marked by artful subtlety and deceptiveness

[796] Secluded – removed or remote from others, solitary

[797] Indefatigable - tireless

[798] Dissembled – disguised

chair from the corner and placed it underneath the aperture[799] in the ceiling. When he stood on it, he could reach the mechanism[800] that opened the trapdoor. He hoisted himself through the opening and into the unknown.

"Nick?" Savannah felt imperiled[801] in the basement all by herself. The hairs on the back of her neck stood up. She wanted more than anything to be out of the dark labyrinth. She theorized[802] how scary it must have been for Dina to be in such a dungeon. Anger seethed inside her at the werewolf who dared to treat her friend this way.

"Come on." Nick interrupted her thoughts of revenge. "Grab my arm. You won't believe where I am."

Savannah climbed on the chair, grasped his arm at the elbow, and held on. Nick hauled her up easily. She fell awkwardly on top of him. They lay there together for a moment to catch their breath. Savannah's could hear Nick's heart thudding. She wished she could stay there for a long moment and have him safeguard[803] her from any future interactions with the werewolves.

Nick gently disengaged[804] her from his chest. "Can you believe it? We're in the library."

They were behind the check-out counter. The trapdoor had been hidden right underneath the stool where Ms. Woodlawn sat.

"Does this mean what I think it means?" Savannah thought of Ms. Woodlawn, straight-laced and brusque[805], and tried to imagine her as a werewolf—a being that acted on instinct and got pleasure from killing. It didn't fit.

Nick spoke the truth, "Ms. Woodlawn is the master werewolf."

Savannah couldn't wrap her head around the idea. Ms. Woodlawn had helped her with countless research projects. She'd never given Savannah any indication that she was anything more

---

[799] Aperture – an opening such as a hole or gap

[800] Mechanism – a system of parts that interacts like a machine

[801] Imperiled – posed a threat to, presented a danger to

[802] Theorized – constructed a theory about

[803] Safeguard – protect

[804] Disengaged – freed or detached oneself

[805] Brusque – abrupt and curt in manner or speech

than an introverted bookworm.

The sudden realization actuated[806] Nick. "Come on, let's go. We've got to find them before they do something awful to Dina."

Savannah set aside her doubts about Ms. Woodlawn. The truth was glaring, and she needed to accept it. "Do you think there's a chance to save her, Nick?"

"There's gotta be." They hustled[807] through the library. Bloody paw prints marked up the hallway. Two sets led from the cafeteria down the hall to the basement entrance. Another set led in the opposite direction toward the exit doors near the student parking lot.

"They must've gone this way." Savannah's hopes grew that it might not be too late for Dina after all.

*

Jenna limped along, following the Master as they loped through the parking lot. The damage from her earlier encounter with Savannah's car had left her less than whole. But with her new powerful body, what might have been a deadly blow was merely an inconvenience[808].

The attack at the school had not been unexpected, but the fact they could be surmounted[809] by a couple of high school kids shocked her and the other slaves. The werewolf clan had believed the hunter would be a formidable[810] opponent[811], but he had been the easy kill.

Too bad that their newest recruit had to be left behind. They'd had no choice. The Master's safety was tantamount[812] to her own. Dragging along an unwilling half-werewolf would only have slowed them down and put the master at risk. Jenna was the Master's only protection now. She was smarter than the boys, but not nearly as strong. Jake and Carter did have that to their

---

[806] Actuated – put into motion or action

[807] Hustled – moved energetically or rapidly

[808] Inconvenience – something interfering with comfort or progress

[809] Surmounted – overcame, conquered

[810] Formidable – difficult to undertake, surmount, or defeat

[811] Opponent – one that opposes another in a battle or contest

[812] Tantamount – equivalent in effect or value

advantage.

She had no sorrow for their deaths. She'd barely escaped one of Nick's silver bullets. She had been more concerned with her job as slave to the Master than the fate of another slave.

The moon shone bright above them, which would make their flight more difficult. The master mentioned a new den somewhere nearby. From there they could convalesce[813], mount a defense, kill their enemies, and disappear from Centerville forever. After the losses they suffered tonight, it would be imprudent[814] to rush into another battle.

Cold air rushed into Jenna's lungs. To run in werewolf form was one of Jenna's favorite things. She could run twice as fast as her human self. With a low center of gravity, she could easily navigate obstacles.

They darted across the busy street, which abutted[815] the school. The Master led her along the wooded edge of the main road. No streetlights shone along this desolate spot of road. They headed toward the small downtown of Centerville. Jenna assumed they'd head into the woods, but it appeared the Master found a den closer to the humans than she'd imagined.

*

Savannah shivered in the bleak parking lot. Daniel's dated van sat miserably in the shadows, the back doors wide open. Earlier they'd been safely ensconced in that vehicle, and Daniel had been alive. An image of dark red blood spilled on the white tile of the cafeteria floor passed before her mind's eye. That hideous[816] memory would never leave her. Not for as long as she lived.

"Savannah, come on, we have to get going." Nick's commanding demeanor calmed her. "We're so close. We can't let them take Dina away from us now."

Despite[817] her gruesome thoughts, Savannah managed to make it to the van. The vehicle was their only hope of catching up to the lightning-fast werewolves. Nick would follow the trail of

---

813 Convalesce – return to health and strength, recuperate

814 Imprudent – unwise or indiscreet

815 Abutted – was next to

816 Hideous – offensive to moral sensibilities, despicable

817 Despite – in spite of, notwithstanding

bloody paw prints, and Savannah would trail him in the van. Even though they now had access to their cell phones, they had no time to explain to the police what was going on. Right now, Savannah barely believed what was going on. She couldn't even imagine trying to explain to the cops. For now, they were on their own.

Galvanized[818] by Nick's encouraging words, she climbed in the front seat. The leopard-print seat covers clashed with the orange shag carpeting, but now instead of being repulsed by Daniel's decorating, she felt a profuse[819] sadness.

Nick had made it to the opposite end of the parking lot. She drove to catch up to him. Nick kicked a vermin[820]-infested pile of garbage near the school dumpsters. His toes prodded one large lump. His shoulders slumped. His whole body changed—his head hung low, and he put his hands in his pockets.

Savannah's heart skipped a beat. The tension ready to explode[821] inside her. He found something, and it wasn't good. Not good at all. An icy claw of fear gripped her.

She pulled up next to him. He stared up into the headlights. He put up a hand, either to block the lights or signal her to stop. She couldn't tell. What had he found there in the heap of trash? He was reticent[822]. His features set in stone. She couldn't read his expression.

Nick approached the van. She rolled down the window.

"Don't come any closer, Savannah." His eyes were dark chasms[823], devoid of all emotion.

Savannah left the engine running. "Why? What is it? What did you find?" she demanded, insistent[824]. She opened her door and pushed against Nick. He blocked her with his body.

Nick shook his head and averted[825] his eyes from her. His hands gripped the doorframe through the unrolled window. "Get

---

[818] Galvanized – aroused to awareness or action

[819] Profuse - plentiful

[820] Vermin – various small animals that are injurious to health

[821] Explode – burst violently as a result of internal pressure

[822] Reticent – restrained or reserved in style

[823] Chasms – a deep, steep-sided openings in the earth's surface

[824] Insistent – firm in asserting a demand or opinion, unyielding

[825] Averted – turned away

back in the van, Savannah." His voice was hollow. "Now."

"Is it Dina?" A strangled cry came from her throat.

Nick's face remained impassive, but the pain in his gaze spoke volumes.

"Tell me, Nick." Hysteria took over. She wanted out of the van. She wanted to see. He had no right to keep her from the truth. "Tell me."

"It's too late for her, Savannah."

Savannah tried to absorb[826] the finality[827] of his words. She slid off the driver's seat and stumbled into the back of the van. She headed for the back doors. "I have to see her." Nick needed to get out of her way.

"No, you don't, Savannah. There's nothing you can do."

She contumaciously[828] made her way out of the van. She needed to see the object next to the dumpster. Nick intercepted[829] her. He was not gentle.

She tottered backward, catching herself before she fell to the pavement.

Nick stood, imposing, in front of her and blocked the view of her friend's ruined body. "Don't." His voice broke. "You don't want to see her like that, Savannah."

She stood for a moment. Her limbs felt stiff and awkward. She caught Nick's gaze and the façade[830] of anger crumbled. He caught her in his arms and held her close for a moment. She clung to him like a boat to its anchor.

"Let's get back in the van," he said gently. "I think they went downtown. I'll drive." He pulled her toward the rusted vehicle.

Savannah stared at the shadowed pile of trash. She wanted to look at Dina's body, but was unable. There were two werewolves left. If they didn't hunt them down tonight, the beasts would continue with their turpitude[831]. They would ravage[832] another life.

---

[826] Absorb – take in

[827] Finality – the quality of being final or definitely settled

[828] Contumaciously – obstinately, stubbornly

[829] Intercepted – stopped or interrupted the intending course of

[830] Façade – deceptive appearance or attitude

[831] Turpitude – depravity

[832] Ravage – bring heavy destruction on, devastate

She couldn't allow that to happen to someone else. She closed her eyes to hold back the tears. She wiped the back of her hand, hard, across her face.

"Yeah, let's go," she said with acerbity[833]. She turned from the scene and climbed into the van.

Nick drove toward the road.

---

[833] Acerbity – a sharp bitterness

CHAPTER SEVENTEEN

Rancor[834] ate away at the Master's sanity. How dare those stupid humans kill two of her slaves and destroy any chances of the newest recruit reaching full werewolf status. The halfling, Dina, had been too weak and too ravenous to bring with them. She most likely would've tried to tear them to shreds, if she and Jenna hadn't killed her first.

A couple of quick, tearing bites to her neck was all it took to get rid of her. A little sanguinary[835], but it had been necessary. Dina would've been a hanger-on[836] who brought absolutely no strength to their small group.

Since Dina had been in the early stages of her transformation, the body they'd left behind had been mostly human-looking. The color and glow in her eyes would diminish quickly after her death. Leaving her body near the dumpster would draw the attention of the many rats that made their home there. The rodents would take care of any other noticeable[837] signs that the girl was anything less than human.

She and Jenna needed to regroup in a new den nearby. Jenna had the absurd[838] notion that they were going to hide out there until morning and make their way to some new place.

---

[834] Rancor – bitter, long-lasting resentment

[835] Sanguinary – bloody, gory

[836] Hanger-on – someone who persistently follows along

[837] Noticeable – evident, observable

[838] Absurd – ridiculously incongruous or unreasonable

The Master had a different plan.

They couldn't be lax[839] and leave those two humans behind. They knew everything about them—their weaknesses and vulnerabilities and how and where they created new werewolves. Nowhere[840] would be safe if those two humans were left alive.

A panacea[841], however, existed for her problem. Tonight was the last night of the full moon. She had a chance to make more slaves. These two. Tonight. Her only slave was wounded; her two strongest slaves had been killed. These two had destroyed her small army, and now they would be the replacements.

*

Jenna had sworn to protect the head werewolf no matter the obstacle or injury. Pain throbbed in her back haunches. She ignored it. The quick pace to their new den was wearisome[842], but the Master pressed on. Even injured Jenna could move more quickly than a human. She scanned the road for their enemies as they navigated[843] through town.

"It's up ahead at the end of the block." The Master directed Jenna's gaze at a cinderblock building huddled near the edges of downtown—a used bookstore. A large plate glass window revealed a quiet interior of bookshelves and comfortable chairs. This should be a secure place to abscond[844] from their enemies and rehabilitate[845] before moving on to a new town and a new life.

The Master led Jenna around the back of the building. Two dumpsters lined the wall of crumbling cinderblock in the alley. The Master kicked an empty cardboard box to one side and revealed a broken basement window. All the glass had been removed. They leapt down into the dank space under the store. Here, they could wait, biding[846] their time until they could make their escape.

*

---

[839] Lax – lacking in rigor, strictness or firmness

[840] Nowhere – not anywhere

[841] Panacea – a remedy, a cure-all

[842] Wearisome – causing physical or mental fatigue

[843] Navigated – made one's way

[844] Abscond – run away, leave quickly and secretly

[845] Rehabilitate – restore to good condition

[846] Biding – waiting for further developments

The basement underneath the bookstore was damp and dark. The Master conceded[847] it was not the best place to conduct the ceremony, but it could be done. "Find some paper, wood, anything that will burn," she ordered her singular slave.

Jenna's glowing eyes narrowed to small slits, "But Master..." The Master struck her slave with a swift and painful blow. "Do it. Now."

How dare a slave question a Master.

Chastened, Jenna averred[848] and slunk away to search for combustible materials.

The Master knew her slave was not pleased with her decision to stay and induct new werewolves into the pack. When instructing her slaves about executing a transformation, the Master had emphasized[849] caution and careful planning. Tonight, however, she had no time for that. She required slaves to keep her safe. She wasn't about to relocate to an unfamiliar place without plenty of protection. This basement would be a quiet place for a few days. She could transform the two students and leave town with a sizeable pack.

She was eager to have that boy as her new slave. Her two toughest slaves may have been lost tonight, but that boy with his intelligence and strength would equal them both.

With the tip of a claw, the Master scratched out a pentagram within a circle on the cement floor. Soon, her newest recruits would arrive. She'd left enough of a trail to ensure they'd find her. Did they really believe a master werewolf would be stupid enough to leave any kind of trail? They had undervalued[850] her mental prowess[851]. They were about to find out how much that mistake would cost them.

*

The van crept down the road, high beams blazing. For the last three or four blocks, Nick and Savannah had been able to follow the slight traces of bloody paw prints on the pavement.

---

847 Conceded – admitted
848 Averred – affirmed positively, declared
849 Emphasized – stressed, singled out as important
850 Undervalued - underestimated
851 Prowess – superior skill or ability

Savannah scanned the macadam[852]. "There, on the right near the curb. Do you see it?"

Meticulously[853], Nick studied the cement curb that lined the edge of the road. "There's a paw print. Guess we're still going in the right direction, then. Let's be scrupulous[854] looking in this area; let me know if you see another one."

Nick's thoughts were scattered. He wanted to concentrate on the discovery of their friend's maltreated[855] body. He knew, though, if he thought too much about her—the blood, the ragged tears in her skin—he would probably drown in his choler[856]. To exact a reprisal[857] on these werewolves, he needed a keen mind. The werewolves might be faster and stronger, but he had a higher degree of acumen and needed to use it to his advantage.

"There's some more, Nick." Savannah pointed.

They neared the small downtown of Centerville, which was comprised[858] of only a few businesses: a bank, a small movie theater, a diner, and a few stores. Before tonight, this part of town held fond memories. Most kids in Centerville saw their first movie here at the Centerville Cinema or ate their first ice cream cone at Dealer's Drugstore on the corner. Tonight the glint of innocence had worn down to a dull sheen.

Nick drove toward the stoplight in the middle of downtown.

After a few more blocks of driving, Savannah sighed. "I haven't seen any prints in awhile now. Let's double back. We might've missed them."

Nick could sense her frustration. "I think we should park and look around. Maybe the prints are getting too faint and infrequent[859] for us to see them from the van."

Savannah agreed.

---

[852] Macadam – paving material

[853] Meticulously – extremely carefully or precisely

[854] Scrupulous – characterized by extreme care and effort

[855] Maltreated – abused, treated in a rough, cruel way

[856] Choler – anger, ire

[857] Reprisal – retaliatory action

[858] Comprised – consisted of, composed of

[859] Infrequent – not occurring regularly

Nick pulled into a <u>parallel</u>[860] spot right outside the bank building. The streetlights lit up the empty street and sidewalks with an eerie orange glow. What once seemed like a <u>peaceable</u>[861] place had turned into a desolate spot, which hid the worst <u>perversity</u>[862] Nick had ever encountered.

Savannah shivered and pulled her jacket more closely about her.

"Where was the last place you remember seeing a print?" The <u>urgency</u>[863] grew within him. He knew the werewolves must be close by. He tried to <u>calculate</u>[864] the <u>mileage</u>[865] in his head.

"About a half-mile back, right before we got to Dealer's." Savannah said.

Dealer's stood only a few blocks down. "Then that's where we'll start." Nick parked the van and grabbed the heavy duffle bag filled with weaponry from the back. He hefted it onto his shoulder. "We'll each need a weapon. There's a couple of good handguns in here."

"I'll take that hunting knife again," Savannah said.

Nick found it hard to believe slim Savannah had killed that werewolf in the cafeteria. Her goal had been good grades and a scholarship only a few weeks ago. Tonight, she was a seasoned werewolf killer. Her steely gaze told him she could kill again, if it came to that.

Nick nodded in <u>approbation</u>[866]. "Let me know if you see anything." They left the van and walked down the middle of the road toward the drugstore in the distance.

"Or hear anything," added Savannah. "In the woods, there was this awful howling. Almost like a scream. You'll know it when you hear it."

Nick took in her warning <u>taciturnly</u>[867] and scanned the road.

---

[860] Parallel – lying in same direction, equidistant in all parts

[861] Peaceable – peaceful, undisturbed

[862] Perversity – deliberately deviating from what is good

[863] Urgency – a pressing necessity

[864] Calculate – ascertain by computation

[865] Mileage – total length expressed or measured in miles

[866] Approbation – official approval

[867] Taciturnly - silently

Her experience with these beasts far outweighed his. The night had been a blur of violence and extraordinary[868] events, poignancy[869] and rage.

"How will we tell Dina's mother?" Savannah broke the silence. "I can't believe it. Dina had been so elated[870] working on the homecoming committee, making new friends…"

"I don't think we'll be the ones to give her the news. Who's going to believe a couple of high school kids anyway? Principal Morgan is going to do his best to cover this up."

"Yeah, I know."

Nick kicked a few loose rocks of asphalt into the gutter. "Look, let's just concentrate on getting through tonight. There's two of those things out there, and we have to make sure they're destroyed."

Savannah clutched the heavy hunting knife to her bosom[871]. The cold weight of the silver blade reassured her in such a contingent[872] situation. "We can do this, right?"

"Right."

Savannah pointed at the last set of prints near the drugstore. They were faded, barely more than a few odd red marks on the edge of the curb.

"I'll go check it out." Nick, emboldened[873] to take the lead, headed across the street. Killing a werewolf with pinpoint accuracy[874] and finding Dina dead had whet[875] his appetite for revenge.

When Savannah opened her mouth to protest, Nick signaled for her to wait and stay quiet. He made his way down a harshly-shadowed alley that led to the back of the building.

*

---

[868] Extraordinary – highly unusual, remarkable
[869] Poignancy – state of deeply felt distress or sorrow
[870] Elated – made proud or joyful
[871] Bosom – chest of a human
[872] Contingent – uncertain because of uncontrollable circumstances
[873] Emboldened – fostered courage or boldness in
[874] Accuracy – precision, exactness
[875] Whet – made more keen, stimulated

Savannah held her breath as the minutes crept by. The cold seeped through her clothes, chilling her from the outside in. The empty street made her feel vulnerable. She sat on the curb opposite the drugstore and gripped the icy cement to await Nick's return. If he found a continuation of the tracks, he'd let her know.

An odd growl-whine filled the air. The hair rose on the back of Savannah's neck. That was the same strange noise from last night in the woods.

Where was it coming from?

She needed to warn Nick, but she worried about revealing his whereabouts[876] . It might put him in danger.

She dashed behind a mailbox for cover. The cold metal against her shivering back provided a modicum of comfort. On the sidewalk she was exposed[877]. Nick in the alley, with no idea danger lurked so near, was in a more unspeakably[878] precarious[879] position. She took deep breaths to slow her racing heart. Panicking would not help. She needed a clear head to figure out what to do or she'd bungle[880] it.

The whining grew from a small, distant noise to a deafening roar.

"Savannah!"

Nick's cry chilled her to the bone.

She heard sounds of a struggle. Without thinking, she leapt up from her crude hiding place and sprinted across the street to the alley.

Those horrible werewolves weren't going to take Nick, too. Not tonight. Not this way.

The sharp zing of a gunshot echoed in the cold night air.

She pumped her legs harder and grabbed her serrated hunting knife. A moonbeam[881] bounced off of its uneven blade. Pure anger, as hot as a conflagration[882], burned inside her.

---

[876] Whereabouts – approximate location

[877] Exposed – with no protection or shield

[878] Unspeakably – beyond description

[879] Precarious – dangerously lacking in security or stability

[880] Bungle – handle badly, botch

[881] Moonbeam – a ray of moonlight

[882] Conflagration – large destructive fire

Savannah yearned to thrust the knife deep into one werewolf and then the next. Thoughts of red and death and violence, of which she didn't think herself capable, filled her mind and reduced her to something barely human. She acted purely on instinct.

She ran into the alley. Uneven shadows concealed the monsters she knew she would encounter there. She vowed she wouldn't stop fighting until her penultimate[883] breath.

*

Nick followed the faint bloody paw prints into the alley. He didn't want to leave Savannah alone in the street, but she'd be safer there. If someone had to encounter a werewolf, he wanted it to be him.

Dina's death had been mind-numbing. He reflected on that moment in front of the dumpsters. His mind didn't fully comprehend[884] the enormity[885] of it. Torn flesh, hair matted with blood, milky eyes open to the moonlit night—it didn't truly look like Dina. Her body appeared more like a mannequin or some special effect from a really good horror movie.

At first, his heart had stopped at the blood and the violence of it. Nick knew, though, that falling into a stupor[886] would help no one. Freezing up at the sight of a his friend's horribly mutilated[887] body would not make the werewolves go away. Once he'd focused on that, he grew more determined than ever to seek out the last remaining creatures. It was imperative[888] to make sure they would never do harm to anyone again.

An odd noise caught his attention. He paused half-way down the alley. In the darkness he lost sight of the tracks. An evanescent[889] flash of movement in the corner of his eye caught his attention.

Nothing but blackness.

---

[883] Penultimate – next to last

[884] Comprehend – get the meaning of something

[885] Enormity – vastness of size, extent

[886] Stupor – a state of mental numbness, a daze

[887] Mutilated – disfigured by damaging irreparably

[888] Imperative – an obligation, a duty

[889] Evanescent – tending to vanish like vapor

Was he delusional[890]?

A screeching growl nearly deafened him. The noise came from all around him. He clapped his hands against his ears to block out the sounds. The gun, gripped in his hand, clunked painfully against his temple.

He swore and realized his error in pointing the gun upward. He swung his arm back down and aimed the gun. His finger tensed on the trigger.

The noise rose and fell all around him. He panicked and turned in a wild circle, aiming the gun at walls and trash and open air.

A rush of breath brushed the back of his neck. Something knocked his feet out from under him, and he fell to the ground. He cracked his head on the cement and tried to get back up. He grew dizzy, and his vision was misty[891].

Two pairs of glowing eyes inched toward him, one step at a time.

He tensed. His heart convulsed[892] painfully, and his limbs froze.

"Savannah!" He shook his foggy[893] head. He had been so heedless[894]. He wanted to tell Savannah to run, to get help, to get away, but the words wouldn't come.

Two enormous creatures appeared out of the shadows, only a few feet from him. The weight of the gun felt heavy in his hand. He'd forgotten he carried the deadly weapon. He slid his finger onto the trigger.

Wait. They're not close enough. Lie still.

The werewolves approached, growling and snapping their raptorial[895] jaws. Nick knew it was a warning to him to remain prone and inert[896].

Hell no.

---

[890] Delusional – suffering from false beliefs, opinions

[891] Misty – vague, hazy

[892] Convulsed – affected with involuntary muscular contractions

[893] Foggy – clouded, blurred, vague

[894] Heedless – thoughtless, unmindful

[895] Raptorial – adapted for the seizing of prey

[896] Inert - unmoving

Nick rose up quick as lightning. He raised the gun and pulled the trigger. He saw a red flash, but it wasn't the impact of the bullet with a furry body. Blood ran into his eyes and hindered[897] his vision. A blast of pain followed.

One of the werewolves had beaten him to the punch and struck him in the head. His bullet had strayed way off its mark, burying itself in the cement block wall.

A shocking wave of pain rippled through his head. He reached up to feel the damage, but an abyss[898] of black overtook him. He thought about Savannah, helpless in the street.

He'd failed her. He'd failed her miserably.

---

[897] Hindered – interfered, obstructed
[898] Abyss – immeasurably deep depth or void

CHAPTER EIGHTEEN

The <u>acrid</u>[899] smell of smoke woke him. Nick jerked up with instincts on alert. <u>Dejection</u>[900] set in as he <u>discovered</u>[901] his wrists tied behind him. His head ached, and the rest of his body felt as if it had fallen from a waterfall onto a <u>plethora</u>[902] of sharp rocks.

A smoldering fire, built from a <u>copious</u>[903] amount of moldy books and newspapers, sat only a few feet away. The fire put out more smoke than flame. He could barely see.

Where was he?

He lay on a hard surface. Cement, possibly. Objects around him were <u>indistinct</u>[904] blobs in the smoky darkness.

How long had he been unconscious? And where was Savannah? Was she safe?

His captors must have noticed his movements because he sensed a presence nearby. A black, furry body slinked up out of the murky darkness, panting hot, stinking breath into his face.

Nick recoiled at the stench.

The werewolf curled its lips back to reveal sharp teeth. Another werewolf stood behind the black one. This one was brownish-gray and smaller.

---

[899] Acrid – unpleasantly sharp, pungent
[900] Dejection – a state of melancholy depression
[901] Discovered – noticed, learned
[902] Plethora – superabundance, an excess
[903] Copious – large in quantity
[904] Indistinct – not clear, faint, dim

Nick tried to decipher[905] if these were people he knew. These two had killed Dina. Even if these were people he'd once known, they were murderers now.

As the black creature hovered over him, Nick could discern a slight change in its appearance. The fur sank into the muscular body, the snout slowly shortened, and the claws rounded into fingernails. In a matter of minutes, Nick no longer saw a werewolf before him, but a human being with queer glowing eyes.

"Ms. Woodlawn." He and Savannah had deduced[906] correctly: the school librarian was the head werewolf. A teacher whom they had trusted had killed Dina. His stomach roiled in unbearable[907] revulsion.

"No need for formalities here, Nick." Ms. Woodlawn's body was human, but her movements were animal. Crouching, she touched his injured head. "I'm sorry about that, but it couldn't be helped."

Nick flinched at the sensation[908] of her cool touch and wanted no sympathy from such a sinister[909] creature.

She dropped her hand. "It should heal quickly after the change." She stood up, took a few steps back, and tilted her head at him, much like a dog would when confused or interested.

That queer look in her glowing eyes, assessing yet piercing, made him shiver. "What are you talking about? What change?" Deep in his heart he knew what she meant.

A slow, wicked smile spread across her usually austere face. "Oh, Nick, I thought you were a lot smarter than that. Isn't that right, Jenna?"

The brown-gray wolf stepped out of the shadows. Jenna Tinsley was the remaining slave. Though her master was in human form, she remained a werewolf. Her left front paw was bloodied and oddly angular[910]. She moved awkwardly.

He kept his gaze on the approaching creature and shifted his

---

[905] Decipher – read or interpret

[906] Deduced – reached by reasoning

[907] Unbearable – so unpleasant or distasteful as to be intolerable

[908] Sensation – the faculty to feel or perceive

[909] Sinister – threatening evil or tragic developments

[910] Angular – having, forming or consisting of an angle or angles

bound hands. The thick, braided rope gave slightly. Or was he merely being too hopeful?

Jenna gave a low growl and showed her teeth.

Although Nick knew there was a teenage girl inside that animal body, he had a hard time believing it.

The smoldering flames burst into a dancing orange fire. The heat grew, and the smoke thickened. Nick coughed. His body went into a spasm. The accretion[911] of light allowed him a better look at where they held him.

Metal shelves on wheels lined the wall in front of him. Behind that, the pattern of cinderblock was visible. He had an inkling[912] he was in some kind of basement or storage area.

"Let's begin." Ms. Woodlawn backed away from Nick.

He sat inside a pentagram circle.

Stealthily[913], he shifted his ensnared[914] wrists back and forth under the rope. The knot slipped. He prayed his captors stayed in front of him. A few more minutes, and he might be able to free himself.

Ms. Woodlawn stepped back into the shadows outside the range of the orange flames. Nick could see her body change. Her perfectly-straight spine curved and lengthened. Her legs and arms morphed into haunches and forelegs. Her head elongated, and fur sprouted. She was human no longer. Two bright-eyed, lithesome[915] werewolves now faced him. The odd whining growl filled the room.

The master werewolf paced back and forth. Nick wondered what they were waiting for. According to Daniel, the head werewolf only needed to bite him, and he would become one of them. Although he worked on the rope around his wrists, it seemed like a fruitless effort. One quick bite, and it would all be over.

The bite didn't come.

The two werewolves paced back and forth as if they were

---

[911] Accretion – an increase by natural growth or addition

[912] Inkling – slight hint or indication

[913] Stealthily – acting with quiet, caution and secrecy

[914] Ensnared - trapped

[915] Lithesome – moving and bending with ease

waiting for something. Or someone.

Savannah.

This had been an ambush[916] for both of them. How could he have been so negligent[917]? He'd been naïve to think it would be this easy to track the creatures down and kill them. His fear for Savannah, instead of petrifying[918] him, pushed him to work even harder to loosen the knots. His wrists throbbed from the constant friction. He knew it wouldn't be long before the tough rope broke his skin. He couldn't stop now, though. He had to liberate[919] himself before Savannah had the same lapse[920] of judgment about the werewolves' cleverness.

*

The moon rose overhead and lit up the alleyway. A puddle of blood stained the ground. Savannah grew sick to her stomach.

Was she too late?

She'd run blindly into the alley, operating on caprice[921]. She hadn't taken the time to think things through the way she usually did. This particular scenario had called for quick thinking. She'd had no time to weigh pros and cons.

She'd expected to be in the middle of a melee[922] and confronted head on by vicious werewolves. When she entered the alley, however, the strange cries had stopped, silence had surrounded her, and Nick was gone.

She succumbed[923] to the fear Nick had been injured by a werewolf. If he'd been killed, she should've found a body. He must've been injured in a skirmish[924], so she should be able to find evidence of his disappearance.

In the bright moonlight, she spied bloody drag marks. They led to the back of the building.

---

916 Ambush – act of lying in wait to attack by surprise

917 Negligent – marked by insufficient care or attention

918 Petrifying – stunning or paralyzing with terror

919 Liberate – free from confinement

920 Lapse – mistake resulting from inattention

921 Caprice – an impulsive change of mind

922 Melee – a violent free-for-all

923 Succumbed – gave up, gave in

924 Skirmish – minor, short-term fight

Nick was still alive.

Steadying the large knife in her sweating palm, Savannah slunk down the alley. She wondered how far two werewolves could convey[925] a body as heavy as Nick's. They might be powerful werewolves, but Nick was no lightweight.

Edging closer to the corner of the building, she listened for any noise to attest[926] that a werewolf waited for her. A cloud shifted over the moon, dimming her view but giving the protection that the darkness could afford her. Her bravado[927] moved her forward. She slipped around the corner, crouched low behind a dumpster and waited.

Nothing came. Only silence greeted her.

She scanned the asphalt beyond the dumpster. The blood trail continued and led right to a broken out basement window.

She knelt and peeked through the opening. In actuality[928], Savannah couldn't see much of anything through the window—a muted orange glow, lots of smoke, and several murky shapes. She backed away. One of the werewolves might spot her. She leaned against the cold metal exterior[929] of the dumpster and took a deep, slow breath. She needed to clear her head and control[930] her fear or she'd fail. She set the hunting knife in her lap and rubbed her sweating palms on her jeans.

She had to do this. Nick needed her. She wasn't going to let him die like Dina.

If she climbed through the window, they would see her for sure. She didn't know if there was another way in to the basement, but she had to find out.

She had ran to the front of the building, her feet barely touching the ground. She'd never sprinted so hard in her life. The dark storefront appeared halcyon[931] in the darkness. Inside,

---

[925] Convey – take or carry from one place to another

[926] Attest – provide evidence for, indicate

[927] Bravado – pretense of courage, false bravery

[928] Actuality - reality

[929] Exterior – external or outward appearance

[930] Control – ability to manage or direct

[931] Halcyon – calm, peaceful, tranquil

bookshelves teemed[932] with neatly arranged books and a tidy counter took up space near the entrance.

Grasping the hilt of the knife, she leapt at the large, plate glass window which protected a display of children's books. Channeling all her hostility[933], she slammed the blunt end repeatedly into the glass. It shattered more easily than she'd expected. So much for secrecy[934] and stealth.
She swept away the sharp shards of glass that remained and knocked down Dr. Seuss books in the window display like a tornado would a forest of trees. Heading straight for a door marked "Employees Only," Savannah gripped her knife, ready for anything.

---

[932] Teemed – abundantly filled
[933] Hostility – hatred, animosity
[934] Secrecy – the condition of being concealed or hidden

CHAPTER NINETEEN

Nick watched his captors carefully. Most of his concentration centered on the laborious[935] task of loosening the ropes around his wrists, but he needed to keep a circumspect[936] eye on the werewolves. They waited for Savannah, and he was determined to do everything he could to intervene[937]. Even if it meant losing his own life in the process.

Suddenly, his bonds gave way. The chafing eased, and he could slip both hands out of the bindings. His exhilaration[938] was short-lived, however. A knot of tension grew in his stomach. Now that he'd freed himself, he didn't know quite what to do. What chance did he have, unarmed, against two powerful werewolves? What had they done with his gun and the duffle bag? If he could only see better in the gloom of the basement, maybe his weapons were closer than he thought.

He focused on the furry bodies in front of him. If he had to, he would use his bare hands to garrote[939] them. The risk to his own life was no longer important. The creatures had to be stopped. He tensed his whole body, wanting to be ready the moment he had an opening for an attack.

A slam echoed through the basement. The werewolves leapt

---

[935] Laborious – characterized by toilsome effort

[936] Circumspect – heedful of potential consequences, prudent

[937] Intervene – get involved so as to alter or hinder an action

[938] Exhilaration – the feeling of lively, cheerful joy

[939] Garrote - strangle

into the darkness, going after the noise. Nick used the opportunity to free himself. He dedicated[940] his focus on his escape. The smoke that curled from the fire made him cough. He tossed aside the loosened ropes got to his feet. He could see the vague outline of a human form near the cement steps in the far corner and the werewolves closing in.

Savannah.

She had no idea about the strength and cunning of her adversaries. Ms. Woodlawn and Jenna had overpowered him easily. If he didn't get to Savannah in time, she would meet the same fate. He had to help her.

He lunged recklessly[941] in her direction, ready to annihilate[942] anything in his path. He tripped and realized he'd stumbled over his duffle bag. His gun lay right on top. The werewolves had made a vital error. Simultaneously[943], he snatched up the gun and dashed to the back of the room, determined to help Savannah.

Savannah stood on the steps, the large hunting knife in her competent[944] hands. The werewolves snarled and snapped at her. The slave werewolf took up a defensive[945] position with the master werewolf behind her. Savannah had distracted them, so they were caught off guard by Nick's approach.

He cocked the gun and aimed at the black fur. The master werewolf wrenched her shaggy head in his direction. Her glowing eyes widened and then narrowed. Her black lips peeled back in a low growl. She tensed her haunches, preparing to leap.

Nick pulled the trigger.

Jenna leapt in front of her master. A high-pitched whine split the air. Jenna knocked the master werewolf forward. Nick's gun went off with a deafening crack, and the bullet missed its mark.

The black werewolf charged forward and knocked Nick to the ground. Her teeth sunk deep into his throat. Nick felt no pain, only incredible pressure. He struggled to breathe. The master's jaws

---

[940] Dedicated – committed to a particular course of action

[941] Recklessly – heedlessly, carelessly

[942] Annihilate – destroy completely

[943] Simultaneously – happening, existing, or done at the same time

[944] Competent – properly or sufficiently qualified

[945] Defensive – carried on in resistance to aggression

clenched down as tightly as a bear trap. A haze came over his vision and then a vortex[946] of blackness.

Someone screamed, but he couldn't figure out why. The sound was distant and oddly muted. A cold, heavy weight in his hand reminded him he had a gun. His arm rose up limply, sloppily. The mordant[947] pressure at his throat turned into a sharpness that inhibited[948] all other sensation, and his hand fell back to the floor.

*

Savannah was in shock. The crumpled body of a werewolf, a long hunting knife sticking from its neck, lay before her on the concrete floor of the basement. Another werewolf, very much alive, gripped Nick at the throat. Exhaustion[949] and terror threatened to pollute[950] her body and render it useless. She ran through a gamut[951] of emotions. What she did in the next few minutes would determine if Nick would survive the night. Everything rested on her shoulders.

Nick lifted his arm lethargically[952], gun in hand.

That kicked her into action. She jumped on the dead werewolf and pried the hunting knife from its bloody, lifeless body. Savannah brandished[953] the knife high over her head and ran at the black, shaggy werewolf holding Nick in its jaws. An animal-like cry ripped from her throat, and she lunged forward for the kill.

The werewolf released Nick and was on her in an instant. The quick reflexes of the supernatural being were no match for a novice werewolf hunter. This *must* be the master werewolf. It moved faster than the werewolves she'd encountered in the high school hallway only hours earlier.

The werewolf's jaws opened. Savannah braced for the bite.

A gunshot rang out.

The black animal slumped on top of her. Its heavy weight

---

[946] Vortex – like a whirlpool or tornado
[947] Mordant – bitingly painful
[948] Inhibited – forbade
[949] Exhaustion – extreme fatigue
[950] Pollute – make unfit for
[951] Gamut – a complete range or extent
[952] Lethargically – without energy
[953] Brandished – exhibited aggressively

pinned her to the cold cement floor. Savannah froze, uncertain what had happened. She pushed at the long, furry forelegs that lay across her chest. The werewolf was most certainly dead.

"Savannah?" Nick gurgled.

"Nick." She pushed the heavy, dead creature off of her.

"Are you okay?" Nick's voice was weak.

She freed herself from the wolfish corpse[954] and crawled to her friend as he bled on the floor. "Oh, Nick." Tears sprung to her eyes. Devastation and grief[955] ached[956] in her chest at the sight of Nick's injury. It didn't look curable[957]. She could hardly believe he was conscious, much less speaking to her. "You need to be quiet." She put a finger to his lips.

Where was her cell phone?

If she didn't call an ambulance in the next few minutes, she was going to lose him. After everything they'd been through, after gallantly[958] jeopardizing[959] his own safety for hers, Savannah was connected to him. The past two days had changed them forever, and she wasn't about to let him slip away.

"I've got to leave you for a minute." She'd seen a phone on the counter upstairs. "I'll be right back."

He grabbed her hand, obstructing[960] her from going anywhere. "No, stay with me. Please."

Strangely, his voice grew stronger and less garbled. Savannah scanned his face. His blue eyes glowed fiercely in the dim room. That otherworldly, unnatural glow. His torn throat healed. The skin knit together as if invisible hands stitched it closed. The blood dried and crusted over in a matter of seconds.

What was happening?

"It can't be." She backed away from him. "It can't be."

Everything Daniel had taught them came back to her. Nick had been bitten by a master werewolf, and then he had killed the

---

[954] Corpse – dead body

[955] Grief – deep mental anguish, intense sorrow

[956] Ached – suffered a dull sustained pain

[957] Curable – being such that healing is possible

[958] Gallantly – bravely, courageously

[959] Jeopardizing – putting at risk

[960] Obstructing – preventing the progress of

master.

Oh, my God.

*

"What is it, Savannah?" Nick felt better. Only minutes ago, he could've sworn he was <u>moribund</u>[961]. He'd lost so much blood that his chance for survival had been slim. But now? In the last few moments an incredible power filled his whole body. His limbs zinged with energy. The once dark and smoky basement was now <u>comparable</u>[962] to a sunny day.

What was going on?

He sat up. In Savannah's eyes he no longer saw concern; he saw fear. "What's wrong?" He flexed his arms. Something was definitely different.

"Your eyes," Savannah whispered.

He knew what was wrong. He knew why he felt so strong, so powerful. The shock made him feel like he'd been <u>submerged</u>[963] into a tank of icy water. The body of the black werewolf lay next to him. That bite had been no ordinary bite. He touched his neck, his gaze locked on the werewolf's still form. Instead of blood and jagged flesh, he felt the smooth plane of his throat, as if nothing had happened.

His stomach became an empty pit.

He was one of them. One of those <u>hybrid</u>[964] creatures.

"What are we going to do?" Savannah's face grew pale.

More than anything Nick wanted to reach out to her, to comfort her after their night of horrors. Was he now one more <u>antagonist</u>[965] she needed to destroy?

The color returned to Savannah's face, and she eyed Nick keenly. "That was the master werewolf?"

"Yes. It was Ms. Woodlawn." Uncertainty grew. Would she go for the knife? Would she get rid of him now before he grew to be a bigger threat?

"So now you're one," she said matter-of-factly.

---

[961] Moribund – approaching death, about to die

[962] Comparable – similar or equivalent

[963] Submerged – put under water

[964] Hybrid – something of mixed origin or composition

[965] Antagonist – adversary, enemy

"I guess so." He felt like Nick, only better. He had no desire to hurt Savannah. If anything, he'd grown more protective of her. "You know I won't hurt you, right?"

His tongue glided over his top row of teeth. There was something different there—something indescribable[966]. He didn't have time to think about what he'd become, so he clamped his jaw together to keep his tongue from its probing[967].

*

Savannah had a hard time looking at him with those unnatural[968] blue eyes. They were hypnotic[969]. Once she stared at him, it was hard to look away. The longer she sat with him, though, the surer she became that he was Nick. He knew who she was. He wasn't going to harm her. Her worries from moments ago seemed inane[970].

"Yes, I know you won't hurt me." She pushed aside any residual[971] fears she had.

He smiled.

"Now what do we do?" They were two dead bodies. Rather than focus on Nick, they needed to concentrate on cleaning up the mess and getting home before dawn. The werewolves—the bad ones--were gone. They'd done their job. They could contemplate Nick's new status later.

Before they could act, the werewolf bodies steamed and smoked. The putrid smell of burned flesh assaulted their nostrils. The bulk of the bodies collapsed inward, as if they were sinking into the floor. Blood, sinew, and bone boiled and hissed, shrinking into ever reducing piles.

Savannah was aghast; Nick was merely observant. His creator and enemy disappeared before their eyes. If the werewolf carcasses[972] no longer existed, what exactly was he? Nick had no

---

[966] Indescribable – defying expression or description

[967] Probing – exploratory action

[968] Unnatural – contrary to nature

[969] Hypnotic – attracting and holding interest as if by a spell

[970] Inane – lacks sense or substance

[971] Residual – a quantity leftover at the end of a process

[972] Carcasses – dead body of an animal

fealty[973] to them, but he also was no longer entirely[974] human.

Savannah grasped his forearm. What good would it do to ask unanswerable questions? The beings who could've helped Nick understand what had happened to him were gone. He and Savannah were the only one who knew. He pulled her to him. The warmth of his body was reassuring.

When the cadavers[975] had vanished into nothing, leaving not even a mark on the concrete, the two of them finally let go of one another. The weak light of dawn filtered through the dusty basement windows, reminding them they needed to be on their way.

Savannah led Nick up the stairs through the silent, neat bookstore—a sharp contrast to the basement's smoky, darkness. They climbed together through the broken window, his hand in hers. She didn't flinch when the tips of his fingernails bit into her palm like claws.

To her, he was still just Nick. Nothing more than that.

---

[973] Fealty – faithfulness, allegiance
[974] Entirely – wholly, completely
[975] Cadavers – dead bodies

CHAPTER TWENTY

Nick drove Daniel's van back to the school. He and Savannah were tired, <u>disheveled</u>[976], and in denial. As they neared the parking lot, they both noticed several police cars, a fire truck, and an ambulance with lights ablaze. Someone must've found Daniel's body and <u>dispatched</u>[977] the authorities to the school.

"Isn't that Principal Morgan's car?" He pointed at the ramshackle Volkswagen near the dumpsters. He felt a <u>slight</u>[978] tug of hope.

"Turn in here." She directed Nick to pull up next to the only person left who might help them.

Nick guided the van toward the little red car without question.

Savannah rolled down her window. The sun had begun to rise up over the bleachers that lined the football field, its orange glow harsh in the clear sky. "Principal Morgan?"

A stoic figure rose up from the heap of trash scattered around the dumpsters. Principal Morgan stood in the very spot where Dina's body had been.

"She's gone," the principal said, as if he expected to see them there. "This was all my fault. I should've exposed what was happening. Explained it somehow."

For the first time since she'd known Principal Morgan, he

---

[976] Disheveled – untidy, unkempt

[977] Dispatched – sent away towards a designated goal

[978] Slight – almost no, very little

was at a loss for words. His usually robust[979] figure was fragile[980] in the pale morning light.

Nick had gotten out of the van. His arms were stiff at his sides. His blue eyes burned brightly in their sockets, like twin supernovas.

She needed to intercept him before he took out his anger on the one man who might be able to help him.

Principal Morgan's eyes widened, perhaps surmising[981] the change in the teenage boy. He backed away from Nick, his hands up in a surrender pose.

Savannah rushed forward. "Nick, wait!" He had to listen to her. He had to stop.

Nick curled his fingers inward toward his palms. His shoulders tensed.

"He can save you," she wrenched out. She needed him to be completely Nick right now. If he couldn't think rationally, act like regular Nick, then maybe there was no point to this at all. He could already be lost to her.

Nick stopped dead in his tracks. He flexed[982] his hands opened and closed several times, as if he were trying to regain his composure.

She stood still, waiting to see what he would do. She grasped the hilt of her knife. "Don't, Nick. Please don't." She didn't know if she'd be able to kill him, but she was prepared to try.

Nick fell to his knees. His put his hands to his forehead[983] and gave a heavy sigh. "I'm sorry. I didn't know what I was…" He shook his head as if it were muddled[984]. He spoke again, his voice much stronger, "It won't happen again."

"It's all right, Nick," Principal Morgan said quietly. His voice shook, but he seemed to be accustomed[985] to the idea that Nick wouldn't hurt him. He turned to Savannah, "You said I could

---

[979] Robust – powerfully built, sturdy

[980] Fragile – frail, delicate

[981] Surmising – infer from incomplete evidence

[982] Flexed - bent

[983] Forehead – part of the face between eyebrows and hairline

[984] Muddled – confused

[985] Accustomed – adapted to

help?"

"That book, the big red one we found in the library. Do you have it?" If there were any way to fix Nick and turn him back into a human, that book would have the answers.

Principal Morgan invigorated[986] when she reminded him of the book. The lines of worry were erased from his face and the edges of his mouth turned up from a solid frown. "In my office. Follow me." He hopped in his car.

Nick, lost in his own morbid[987] thoughts, was hard to rouse. "Nick, come on. I think we can help you."

Nick's gaze was like a laser beam, even in the bright morning sun. Savannah shivered. She hid her fear from him by smoothing her hair back. She knew his new werewolf senses picked up on the slight movements because pain and fear were abundantly[988] visible on his face. That hurt her to the very core.

She reached out her hand to him. His gaze was full of doubt. He gripped her proffered[989] hand. They walked to the car with their hands conjoined[990].

"Do you think the book can really help me? Do you think there's a cure?" The plea in his voice broke Savannah's heart.

"I won't give up until we find something, Nick. I promise you."

They drove the short distance from the far end of the parking lot to the curved driveway at the school's front entrance. The ambulance had left. Only two police cars remained on the scene. If the other werewolf bodies had disintegrated like those in the basement, the only corpse the police had discovered was Daniel's.

Principal Morgan was outside the school. He was talking to a police officer who stood by the only outside access[991] to the school office.

After a few moments and a flash of I.D., the officer waved

---

986 Invigorated – made lively

987 Morbid – suggesting the horror of death and decay

988 Abundantly – abounding with, rich

989 Proffered – presented for acceptance or rejection

990 Conjoined – united, made contact, came together

991 Access – a way of entering or leaving

Principal Morgan through the office door. Principal Morgan gave Nick and Savannah a hard stare that seemed to say, "Wait here." Savannah could tell Nick was anxious to get his hands on that book. In a few hours their families would be waking up and looking for them. She hoped he could go home with the knowledge that an antidote[992] for his condition existed.

Nick nudged her in the side and pointed at the principal as he sauntered out of the door with a myriad[993] of manila folders stacked in his hands. Underneath the folders, Savannah recognized the familiar tooled red leather binding.

He had the book.

Savannah's heart raced. She wouldn't lose another friend to the clutches of the werewolves. Nick would be safe.

If only they had been able to save Dina, too.

Principal Morgan approached the van. Savannah rolled down her window. He passed the heavy book to her. "If there's anything you need, anything I can do…" To hear the tough-as-nails principal vow to help them was nothing less than astonishing. Savannah's earlier conclusions[994] about him were so inaccurate. All along this man had wanted to help his students. He may have made some mistakes, but overall, he really had done what he thought was best for the school and the kids.

Savannah laid the heavy book in her lap. "Thanks."

Nick gave Principal Morgan a substantive[995] handshake. The gossamer[996] strand of trust they'd built only moments before was strengthening. They eyed one another, both knowing the prognosis[997] for his future was uncertain.

"Let's go home," Savannah said wearily.

"You got it."

Savannah rolled up her window to keep out the chill of the morning air. Even with the heat blasting through the vents, she had an uncontrollable shivering that came from deep within. She

---

[992] Antidote – an agent that relieves or counteracts

[993] Myriad – a vast number

[994] Conclusions – judgment or decision reached after deliberation

[995] Substantive - solid

[996] Gossamer – something light delicate or flimsy

[997] Prognosis – the likelihood of recovery from a disease

wanted to forget last night, forget about Dina's death, forget about what Nick was becoming. After a few hours' sleep she'd be able to focus again and figure out what to do.

Savannah leaned back in her seat and closed her eyes to the burning, morning rays of the sun. What she needed right now was rest.

EPILOGUE

Savannah was asleep next to him. Nick could sense the slight changes in her body—the relaxing of her arms, the slowed pace of her breathing, even the subtle change in her body position. His new abilities were astonishing and frightening, and he didn't plan on sharing them with Savannah yet. He wanted to allay[998] any fears she may have about him, not give her more reasons to distrust him.

Nick pulled up to a stoplight. They were the only vehicle at the intersection. The silence in the van was so absolute that he reached for the radio. Any sound would be better than the silence.

A driving, gnawing pain hit his stomach with the force of a sixteen-wheeler plowing into a brick wall. He gritted his teeth together to keep from screaming. He doubled over the steering wheel and clutched at his abdomen.

My God. What was happening?

The pain was intolerable. The hair on the back of his neck rose up. Sharp, stabbing pains ran up and down his body, radiating from his stomach. They were the most voracious[999] hunger pangs imaginable. As if he hadn't eaten in weeks.

The pain subsided as soon as it began. He let out a huge sigh.

"The light's green," mumbled Savannah sleepily.

Nick grunted a response.

She shifted in her seat, and her eyes slit open. "Are you all

---

[998] Allay – calm or pacify
[999] Voracious – devouring or craving food in great quantities

right, Nick?"

For several seconds he said nothing. He lifted his head from the steering wheel, pressed down on the gas pedal, and drove through the intersection toward Savannah's house.

"I'm fine." He looked at her, her relaxed body warm next to him. "Just fine." He smelled the rich warm blood within her veins and realized with horror that he wanted to taste it.

"Do you want to stop to get something to eat?" she asked quietly, sleep elusive even though she must be exhausted.
"Yeah," Nick said. "I'm <u>famished</u>[1000]."

[1000] Famished – extremely hungry

ABOUT THE AUTHOR

K. J. Gillenwater survived life as a military linguist and a technical writer before pursuing her dreams to become the novelist she'd wanted to be since grade school. She writes what she loves: suspense and romance with a paranormal twist. When she isn't writing, K. J. loves to watch way too much T.V., bake, hang out with her family and enjoy the view from her front porch.

If you enjoyed this book, K. J. Gillenwater is the author of two paranormal suspense books, which are available in print and in eBook format through Amazon, Barnes & Noble and other online retailers.

The Ninth Curse

His blood for a cure. It's a cruel and deadly bargain…

Nine curses. Nine weeks to live. Joel Hatcher has inherited more than a family legacy. It's a time bomb that's ticking down to the inevitable: his own death. But the curse won't die with him. Unless he can find a way to break the cycle, his younger brother becomes the next victim.

In the throes of the third curse, the Painful Pox, Joel makes a last-ditch decision to seek the help of a young spiritualist.

One look into Joel's suffering eyes, and "Madame Eugenie" finds herself torn between doing the right thing and fulfilling her most secret wish—bring her husband Adam back from the dead. Joel's cursed blood is the missing ingredient in her resurrection rituals, and Adam's spirit whispers seductively that there's only one way to get it: steal it.

As Gen and Joel unearth his family's past to track down a cure, they come closer to each other, and to a horrible truth. To live, Joel must lose everything. Including the woman he has grown to love.

Warning: This book contains curses, sacrifices, a ghostly husband, a crazy cat and a love that defies all odds.

The Little Black Box

After the suspicious suicides of several student test subjects, Paula Crenshaw, research assistant and budding telekinetic in Paranormal Sciences at Blackridge University, suspects they may be connected to a little black box designed to read auras. Professor Jonas Pritchard, the head of the department, doesn't believe his precious experiment could be causing students to drop like flies.

But when her best friend almost dies after her encounter with the black box, Paula is certain there is a connection. She pulls her cute, but sloppy, office buddy, Will Littlejohn, into the mystery, and they get closer to the truth behind who might be financially backing the project and why. Haunted by memories of a childhood accident, which she believes she caused with her untamed psychic abilities, Paula finds herself lured to the black box and its mysteries.